ALBERTO ALESSI

Overall Coordination
Renato Sartori, Marco Marabelli

Editor
Stefano Zuffi/Electa, Agnese Piana/Alessi

With the collaboration of
Gloria Barcellini, Ausilia Fortis,
Grazia Pagani

With thanks to
Lowe Lintas Pirella Göttsche,
Sottsass Associati, Studio Quadrifoglio,
Patrizia Scarzella,
Isabella Gianazza, Tatjana Pauli,
Rossella Savio, Gail Swerling

Cover Illustration
The Merry-go-round, drawing by Alessandro Mendini, 1999

Cover Design
Marco Marabelli

Translation
Adam Victor for *Scriptum*, Rome

www.alessi.com

Contents

Introduction

● Since time immemorial the Alessi family has been firmly established on Lake Orta. We originally come from Luzzogno, the oldest village in the Strona valley. The first Alessi I've traced was called Giovanni; in 1633 he married a certain Caterina Gozano in Luzzogno. That's all I know about him, and I don't know a great deal more about the eight generations separating him from me. I nonetheless have no doubt that my forebears were among the

many men from the Strona valley who, in the seventeen hundreds, went as far as Germany to learn the trade of pewter-maker. Some of their number stayed on to make their fortune; others returned home and opened the first craft workshops. Such were the beginnings of the Omegna (and its suburb Crusinallo) makers of metal household objects, today one of the most dynamic centres in Europe for the production of such items.

▲ Six members of the Alessi family, each with one of our most famous "mystery objects", Philippe Starck's *Juicy Salif* lemon squeezer. Sitting in the centre is Carlo; behind him, his brother Ettore, son Michele and nephew Stefano; sitting to his left is his son Alessio. I'm the one in the foreground.

▲ The blue expanse of Lake Orta from above. Right, the outline of *Anna G.*, the character created by Alessandro Mendini as a corkscrew, watching over the Crusinallo plant.

▲ In the Strona valley, between the slopes of Monte Rosa and the lake, traditions retain a tenacious grip: a new museum, the Omegna Forum, gathers together the moving testimonies of centuries of toil and poetry.

The first metal household article manufacturer in the Cusio area was a man called Baldassare Cane, who towards the mid-eighteen hundreds had the courage to leave Chesio (another small village in the Strona valley) for the lakeside and found the first true workshop. Although the company no longer exists, by around 1900 it was a large employer. In the following years his example was followed by many dozens of craftsmen/small businessmen, who often learned their trade as workmen at Cane's factory. Over the course of one and a half centuries, pewter has given way to other metals: brass, nickel silver, aluminium and then stainless steel, whose cycle of development is still running its course. Yet during this period neither the type nor the nature of the objects themselves have changed, and my town remains dominated by this industrial specialization. Along the shores of Lake San Giulio, amongst the Romanesque churches and the Baroque chapels, the household goods factories have become a precise point of reference, leaving their strong social and cultural imprint on the whole area. One of those early craftsmen/small businessmen was my grandfather, Giovanni Alessi. This book sets out to tell the tale of how a deep-rooted, hard, traditional and perhaps even inward-looking manufacturing tradition has blossomed into our own business venture, on the contrary characterized by constant innovation, open to experimentation and to the paradoxical results of casting from a poetic mould. How Alessi has changed from being a "Workshop for the working of brass and nickel silver plates, with foundry" (so read the sign over our stand at the first Milan Trade Fairs in the twenties) into one of the "factories of Italian design". The change from a metallurgical and mechanical industry into a workshop actively researching the field of applied arts has been

a gradual one over several decades. It has been an exciting process which, quite possibly, could serve as a possible model for the evolution of many kinds of industry in our consumer society. This too is a reason to read on.

▲ The *Omegna Tablet in Orthographic Characters*, designed by Luigi Serafini in 1985, is a wry, pseudo-archaeological look at the "meaning" of Alessi and its history.

The 1920s and 1930s

▲ FAO, or Fratelli Alessi Omegna: the overlapping letters of the first historic logo with vaguely deco curves.

▼ Company founder Giovanni Alessi began as a particularly skilful maker of brass knobs.

● Grandpa Giovanni was a talented sheet-metal worker. In 1921 he bought a plot of land at Omegna and founded Alessi. He started handmaking objects for the table and for the home in copper, brass and nickel silver, which were then either nickel-, chrome- or silver-plated. Grandpa was a real stickler for quality and for work well done: the things he made quickly won acclaim for their workmanship and perfect finish.

▲ Something of an epicure, Grandpa came away from long meals with inspiration for new objects. Here he is with his friend "Cichin" Lagostina.

▶ An engraving of the old factory at Crusinallo, set in the Alpine foothills. Today the scene looks like an industrial archaeological landscape.

 ◀ The first items produced by Alessi were inspired by the canons dictated by the most famous household goods companies at the start of this century, particularly Austrian and English factories. The materials (brass and nickel silver) are typical of household preferences during the twenties.

▲ Alessi in the early days: the cleaning department. Items were manufactured to order, according to the specific requirements of the customer —a way of working still based on a crafts approach.

▲ Engravings in the early catalogues are a time machine back to middle-class tastes of the day.

▶ An interesting example of a typical—now extinct—object on Italian tables between the two wars: a *Flask holder* (1925).

▼ Double services (teapot, coffee pot, sugar bowl and milk jug on a tray) are the mainstay of output.

ALESSI

▶ Starting in 1924 the Fratelli Alessi Omegna company began manufacturing coffee pots and trays, as well as small household items.
Still no pots and pans or cutlery, items requiring more complex materials and processing.

▲ The illustrations on these pages are based upon some of the objects found in the oldest Alessi catalogues, as reinterpreted by air-brush artist Tiger Tateishi in 1979.

▶ The quality of Giovanni Alessi's household articles improved rapidly, thanks to technical innovations such as chroming by galvanic bath, nickel-plating and silver-plating. These objects had the no-nonsense solidity of everyday common sense, finished with delicate and traditional ornamental elements.

◀ As Alessandro Mendini points out in his 1979 book *Paesaggio casalingo*, until the thirties developments within the company took the form of an analytical building up of standard objects. The catalogues (the earliest of which dates back to 1925) mark the start of an autonomous activity, showing a dense succession of crafted articles for coffee and tea, for the table, bars, and kitchens, corresponding to a highly polite and archaic way of eating. Objects of this kind are important more for sociological than aesthetic reasons; they have entered our collective past and our collective memory.

Carlo Alessi

◀ The ALessi FRAtelli eagle brand logo took flight in 1947, replacing the old FAO acronym; it was to stay in use until 1967, when it gave way to the Cesalleria Alessi brand.

◀ The *Octagonal tea and coffee service* was a de rigeur presence in the possessions of a "proper family" (1935).

● Design, as we understand the word today, first made its appearance with my father, Carlo. Trained as an industrial designer in Novara, he joined the company when still very young, dedicating himself to design right from the start. He was responsible for most of the objects made between the mid-thirties and 1945, the year he launched his last project, that archetype of early Italian design, the *Bombé* tea and coffee sets.
In the fifties he took over from Grandpa at the helm of the company, completely giving up (I have never understood why...) design.

▲ In the fifties my father (here strolling with Leo Oggioni, our first agent for Italy) transformed Alessi from a small business to a true industrial concern, dynamically expanding exports to encompass over sixty countries.

During the war years, as the household goods market slowed down, Alessi produced stars for uniforms and mechanical parts for Savoia Marchetti aeroplanes. After the war, faced with an enormous demand for brass ladles for the U.S. army, my father doubled the number of machine tools, expanded the company and started mass-production. As he had realized so early, stainless steel was set to conquer the space vacated by chromed metals and silver-plated alloys.

◄ An overhead view of the *Oil cruet* and *Cheese cellar*, two 1949 prototypes which were initial experiments into a new alloy with a great future ahead of it: stainless steel.

ALESSI

The 1950s and 1960s

▼ Carrying on from the preceding decades under Ettore Alessi's technical guidance, the major push into the catering market: the handles and spouts in the *Dani* service (1963–98) are longer and more pronounced, as if to mirror the personality of objects which though practical are certainly not anonymous; the range includes coffee jugs and cream jugs.

● Uncle Ettore, eleven years younger than his brother, joined my father in 1945. Although he no longer officially works for the company, he remains the great authority on cold pressing of metals. I affectionately refer to him as our "mega-technical director". As head of the technical department, in 1955 he opened Alessi up to collaboration with external designers; working with architects Carlo Mazzeri, Luigi Massoni and Anselmo Vitale the result was several ranges of objects, particularly for the catering trade, many of which are still big sellers.

▲ The wire *Citrus basket*, in production from 1952, is a veritable "industrial standard"; it symbolizes our fifties output.

▲ The community service designed around the *101* coffee pot, in production since 1956, numbers twenty-eight different objects, and is the most professional and most popular line in the company's history.

▲ The introduction of stainless steel processing brought a number of structural and technical changes to the company.

▼ Ettore Alessi strengthened the design identity of the company's technical office, paving the way for development of several best-selling products such as the range of wire *Baskets* and *Fruit bowls*. He oversaw a radical new shift in materials: brass and nickel silver made way for stainless steel, the new king of the household, first brought experimentally to Alessi by Carlo in the late thirties.

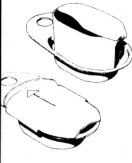

▲ A project approach means blending the artistic freedom of the designer with the concrete requirements of manufacturing. Inevitably, some ideas are destined not to progress beyond the design stage, such as this double *Sauce-boat* designed by Joe Colombo and Ambrogio Pozzi.

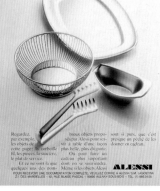

▼ Massoni and Mazzeri's objects are part of *Programme 4*, a cultural shift which introduced the concepts of "designer", "project" and indeed "design" to the world of household articles.

▶ In 1957, as part of the debate on the evolution of applied arts and nascent industrial design, the *Shaker*, *Ice bucket* and *Ice tongs* from *Programme 4* were selected and displayed at the 11th Milan Triennale Exhibition. For the first time, Alessi articles appeared in an exhibition on "designer" industrial production.

ALESSI

▶ The *Avio* (1961–98) series includes the tray pictured below. The name is not only a tip of the hat to airline companies, it is a homage to Alessi's history: mass manufacture in the 1950s was only possible because of supplies from aeronautics parts suppliers during the Second World War.

▼ In this "pre-'68" advertisement the Eiffel Tower is a rather ingenuous, but nevertheless explicit, signifier: internationality and class. Alessi steel articles gleam on a swish terrace, counterpoised perhaps involuntarily, but most certainly effectively, against the most spectacular modern symbol of metal use.

The 1970s

● Officially my career at Alessi began in July 1970, the day after I graduated in law. My dad immediately set me to work on new projects. I threw myself into the job. With a strongly utopian view of "multiplied art", I developed my own brand of cultural-theoretic manifesto championing a new commercial civilization offering the consuming masses veritable artistic items at low prices.

▲ The designers signed up for the "art multiples" were Italian sculptors Giò Pomodoro, Carmelo Cappello, Pietro Consagra and Andrea Cascella, with Yugoslav Dušan Džamonja. The process was a kind of collective madness which tied up our mechanical workshop for almost three years. Staring at the Salvador Dalí prototype my father decided the moment had come to pull the plug on the escapade: but I had already bought the 50,000 steel hooks to manufacture the first 1000 multiples.

◀ Franco Sargiani and Eija Helander are the first designers I brought to Alessi. The partnership with them extended to graphic design, packaging and stand design, as well as the Crusinallo offices. Attempting to rationalize fundamental aspects of corporate life was a huge job. The new *Alessi* logotype began to be used in 1971.

▲ Here the Alessi stands designed by the Sargiani-Helander duo in the early seventies.

▲ The company offices at Crusinallo are also a Franco Sargiani collaboration.

▶ My brother Michele's home at Suna (1981) is, in my opinion, one of the best projects Franco has done for us.

▼ A strong bond grew with the extrovert and enthusiastic Franco. Development of *Programme 8* took five years. The basic idea: total component mobility of basically square or rectangular objects, which were difficult to manufacture in steel. A true international innovation in household objects in the seventies, it was backed up by a major advertising campaign.

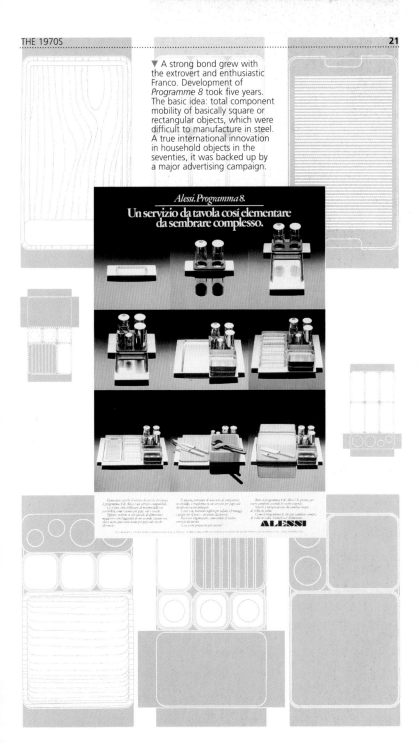

◀ In 1972 Sargiani accepted the request to introduce me to some top designers to launch *Programme 7*. The first contacts were with the Milan-based Exhibition design group. Under the leadership of Silvio Coppola (left), Pino Tovaglia, Franco Grignani, Giulio Confalonieri and Bruno Munari all worked for us, though the resulting designs didn't ever see the light of day. With hindsight, I recognize that those objects still belonged to 1960s style "Bel design Italiano".

▲ The *Tiffany* tray (1974–97) symbolized the range: 10,000 items per year, and a turnover which cheered the intolerant and ferocious Coppola. Sales this big were of huge importance to me: I had proved that designer items could sell well! It was around that time that Dad started going fishing every Thursday.

◀ Coppola's baskets and trays combine tightly packed graphic analysis complete with minuscule handwritten notes, and an innovative use of technological research. His work focused on finding new ways to perforate and shape steel sheeting, wire and gratings. This series had a tough genesis, particularly because of how complex it was to mount the objects, but the public response was extremely encouraging: Tovaglia's *Teorema* tray (1973, out of production), Confalonieri's *Maya* basket (1977) and Coppola's *Square* basket (1977) provided us with a balanced and in its own way classic form of high quality "modern" which was by no means too extravagant.

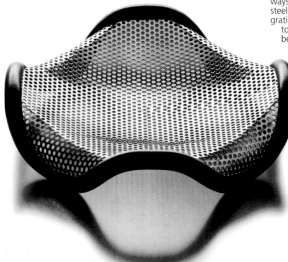

Ettore Sottsass

" I think it is very hard to design a 'beautiful table': it does not depend simply on the tools and materials one uses, it depends on a subtle, fragile and uncertain sagacity which, sometimes, somebody—who knows how and who knows why— manages to channel into the design: a total perception of our cosmic adventure, as fleeting, ineffable and incomprehensible as it may be. "

● Ettore Sottsass came to Crusinallo in 1972, on Sargiani's invitation. Uncle Ettore and I met him; I was really impressed. He was preceded by the fame of his work for Olivetti, his reputation as the guru of radical design… and he was the first person of truly international standing with whom I had dealings. He is something of a philosopher, bursting with charisma, and he has something interesting to say about everything. It was with him that I began talking over the "high" topics of design, the role of industry in society. Although we meet up only once in a while— due to a certain shyness on my part, as if I was afraid of using up the relationship with him— he was the first person I met through work who for me has become a real mentor, one of my maestros.

▶ One truly unique range: the professional articles for the bar and for serving wine, designed by Sottsass in 1979 with assistance from Alberto Gozzi, taking a cue from the perfect cocktails prepared with such expertise by David Niven in those fifties movies.

▼ The range takes its name from the American shaker (Boston), and includes the *Wine cooler* in two versions (for Bordeaux style or for magnums), supplied— if requested—with a special *Stand*, *Strainer*, *Ice tongs* and *Stirrer*.

▶ A homage to Gauguin intimated in this ad conveys the impression that Sottsass's *Holder and oven-to-table porcelain dish* is an instant classic: technical and stylistic details in common with the *5070* condiment set.

▼ Sottsass does not discriminate between materials: he is one of the most prolific designers in wood, as in his late eighties Twergi line.

▼ The *Tray*, or to be precise the rectangular "fancy tray" (1982) is a subtle Sottsass jibe at Alessi; he well knows how challenging it is to manufacture stainless steel in boxy shapes.

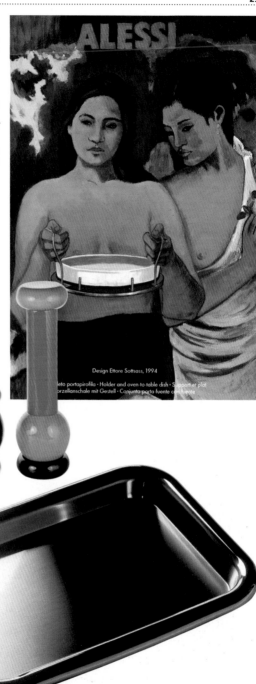

Design Ettore Sottsass, 1994

...leto portapirofila · Holder and oven-to-table dish · S...port et plat
...orzellanschale mit Gestell · Conjunto porta fuente con fuente

A L E S S I

◀ The first items Sottsass designed for Alessi were large, wide-rimmed trays: we quickly decided that was not the right direction, and we asked him to tackle oil cruets. With his Finnish assistant Ulla Salovaara he soon came up with the *5070* condiment set (1978), one of our best designs of the last twenty years, and certainly one of our articles that comes closest to being an "industrial standard". Despite being relatively expensive, this little table-top mosque is our best-selling steel condiment set.

▲ *La Bella Tavola* porcelain service saw the light of day in 1993. Sottsass designed this in pure white lines, or in a version with subtle, classic, overlapping blue lines.

▶ His curiosity piqued by the idea, and by the broad spaces left on the ornamental edges, Alighiero Boetti, one of Italy's most original contemporary artists, came up with an elaborate decoration unique in its use of a plethora of shapes and colours.

▲ Ettore has the greatest
number of designs in our
catalogue. His wish, shared
by Alessi, is over time to build
up a complete family of objects
for the table and the kitchen, as
did Josef Hoffmann for Wiener
Werkstätte.

▶ Sottsass is also the man
responsible for the first Alessi
Flagship in Milan (1982),
refurbished in 1999 by the
Atelier Mendini (see the chapter
"The Wonder Shop").

▲ The *Ginevra* range of crystal glasses is dedicated to the pleasures of "fine drinking". As well as glasses and goblets of varying sizes, there is also a *Decanter*, so beloved of the connoisseur.

▼ Designed in 1987, with the assistance of Alberto Gozzi, the *Nuovo Milano* cutlery set has become a classic, winning the XVIth Compasso d'oro award.

▲ Sottsass's ambition is becoming a reality: to design an entire table place setting, *a very gracious way of demonstrating awareness, respect and care for the* basic *event of nutrition*.

ALESSI

▼ For many years I had wanted to tackle very basic objects, such as these *Castors* (for sugar, salt, cocoa powder, cheese, pepper, chili pepper etc.) and *Butter dishes*, inspired by the static nature of the pictures of American painter Edward Hopper. Ettore did things his own way, forsaking glass for PMMA covered in delicate see-through hues through which the contents may be glimpsed (1998).

▶ The big *Sugar bowl* and spoon, in steel and plastic, is also from 1998.

▼ In the flood of objects Sottsass has designed for Alessi, rare have been his forays into the coffee world: but in the shadow of the smoking totem of a coffee pot (not his, because we don't have any of his in production as yet, but there's still Sapper, Rossi, Graves, Dalisi or King-Kong...), here is his *Sugar and cream set*, with a tray, a blue sugar bowl plus sugar spoon, and a white cream jug (1998).

Richard Sapper

" No, the Japanese are not a threat; they don't have garages... "

● Richard first came to Crusinallo on Shrove Tuesday, 1977. Ettore Sottsass recommended him in these terms: *He's the Tizio lamp guy, the guy who has never done a bad design.* Dad, Uncle Ettore and I greeted him. He was dressed all in black and wearing a bizarre piper's hat. Sapper usually works on just a few designs at a time, only things that really interest him; it's hard to force him into a narrow brief: far better to give him free reign, at a rate of roughly one new project every five years.

▲ Sapper has designed some items which have become historic not just in design terms, but also for Alessi's economic fortunes: the *9090* coffee pot (next page, above). Launched in 1979, this was Alessi's first project for the kitchen; until then we had focused only on objects for the dining and living room.

ALESSI

▲ Two flagship Sapper designs for Alessi: coffee pot *9090* (the first coffee pot manufactured at Crusinallo, awarded the XIth Compasso d'oro and on display at the MoMA in New York), and the majestic *Kettle with a singing whistle*, inspired by the sound of the steamers and barges that ply the Rhine, the first "designer" kettle (1982).

◄ The *Kettle* is characterized by two pitch-pipes in "E" and "B" lodged in the brass whistle pipes. Small devices commonly used to tune musical instruments, they are specially made for us by craftsmen in the Black Forest.

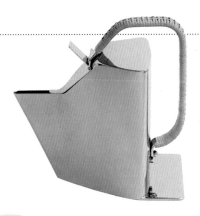

▶ A real thorn in the side of our engineers, Sapper's presence in the company has to be carefully regulated to prevent sparks flying. In the best Ulm school tradition—"the designer must, by definition, know the technology he works with intimately"—Sapper considers himself an expert on every manufacturing topic: because of the countless hard-to-make details in his designs, he gets into long and hotly contested arguments with the engineers. The results are stunning: the *Bandung* "automatic" tea maker, (produced from 1995 to 2000) and his most recent project, the *Cobán* electric coffee maker, which aroused the same feelings in me when I saw its earliest prototype as the *9090* coffee pot did, twenty-one years ago.

◀ The *Cobán* (1997) was launched in four versions to cater to the personal tastes of vast numbers of coffee drinkers. The two traditional versions (with and without coffee grinder) are joined by two innovative ones using pre-packed easy-to-use coffee doses: the *Nespresso*, which uses proprietary coffee portion doses, and the *Easy Serving Espresso*, which takes E.S.E. single use coffee portions (both 1998).

ALESSI

Sapper is also the man behind the most complex project I have ever worked on: the *Cintura di Orione* range of cooking utensils, made possible thanks to Professor Alberto Gozzi's fundamental help and designed to accommodate the suggestions of several famous French and Italian chefs and experts in European cookery. The research project, begun in 1979—now available in a historical volume—was dedicated to a group that, until then, had been somewhat neglected by the market: "private gourmets", people with a passion for inventive and creative cookery.

LA CINTURA DI
ORIONE

▶ **Roger Vergé**

Blending innovation and tradition, he finished off the unusual large oval-shaped *Fish poacher with rack* (60 centimetres long), ideal for cooking fish of varying sizes, as well as pig's trotters.

◀ **Thuilier & Charial**

The godfather of French cuisine was a consultant on the *Oval casserole*, a cast iron pot ideal for slow cooking stews and braised meats. The strong material and heavy lid keep in all the steam and flavours.

▶ Pierre and Michel Troisgros

The Lyon-based masters in Nouvelle Cuisine
worked on the *Black-iron frying pans* (curves
specially designed to facilitate omelet flip
acrobatics), the *Long-handled saucepan*,
and the delightful single-serving *Cassolette*.

▼ Gualtiero Marchesi

The Italian "creative chef"
par excellence worked on the
more traditional items, such
as the *Stockpot* and the two
copper and steel *Casseroles*.

ALESSI

◀ **Angelo Paracucchi**

A great exponent of Mediterranean cooking, worked with Sapper on the *Flambé pan* and *Lamp*, objects right out of the spectacular traditions of the Belle Époque, re-invented in a modern interpretation.

▶ **Alain Chapel**

The undisputed international authority on sauces worked on the copper and steel *Sauteuse* with flared sides, adding a *Whisk* for beating and mixing.

◀ **Alberto Gozzi**

Alberto Gozzi (wearing the eyeglasses), an expert gourmet, and teacher of advanced courses for catering school teachers, has worked as a gastronomical advisor on many Alessi projects.

He was also coordinator of the research that led to this range of utensils. A few years ago he was "pinched" by the Italian President, who summoned him to Rome to run the catering at the Quirinal Palace. A richly deserved promotion.

Achille Castiglioni

❝ *Naturally, Alessi design concept is so broad that there was just the right space and positioning for my own design concept. And I feel great in this space... this element of enjoyment is an integral part of both my own and Alessi's design.* ❞

● I clearly remember the first time I met this great legend of Italian design, Castiglioni, in his Milan studio at Piazza Castello: we soon worked out a possible area of collaboration, the *Dry* service range of cutlery. I consider Castiglioni a great master, a man of insatiable curiosity, blessed with great irony and exceptional modesty; a man who can design masterpieces. He is very realistic, like the good Milanese gent he is, and he understands his audience well. The best way to get him to work is to bring him an idea that tickles him. Our best ideas have come to us late in the evening, over a tumbler of whisky.

▶ The three Castiglioni brothers in sporting garb, in a drawing/caricature from the thirties.

▼ The *Fruit bowl-colander* (1995) responds to two fundamentals for Castiglioni: providing a practical solution to small "dining at table" problems, where possible with a small but intelligent functional innovation, plus the people's preference for a polished metal finish. In a broad Milanese accent, Castiglioni sums up: *cinc ghèi pussée, ma luster* (*five lire more, but shiny*).

◄ To solve the *Ash-tray* conundrum—torment and delight of many a designer—Castiglioni, an absent-minded smoker, provides an ingenious solution: a spiral spring (easy to extract for cleaning) holds the cigarette and prevents it from falling (1970).

▲ Over thirty years separate the two designs in this photo, both manufactured in 1996: the *Ondula* fruit bowl and *Firenze* wall clock, designed with his brother Pier Giacomo for the 1965 "La casa abitata" exhibition held at Palazzo Strozzi, Florence.

▲ *Wristwatch*, created with the graphic input of Max Huber for the dial, in production between 1988 and 1993.

▶ *Foldable tray*, with retractable sections to vary its dimensions, never went into production (1982).

A L E S S I

◄ These glasses are another classic project begun with brother Pier Giacomo: the original design dates back to 1960, but Achille has updated it, and come up with some new items, after collaborating with well-known wine and food expert Luigi Veronelli, whose responsibility also runs to the name *Orseggi* (1997).

▼ The *Splügen* beer glass and bottle opener are a 2001 reproduction of two classic Castiglione designs, produced originally in 1960 for the Splügen Bräu bar project in Milan.

▲ The *Grand Prix* cutlery set won first prize
in the competition held by Gio Ponti for
Reed & Barton in 1960, but never produced,
probably because of the extreme technical
complexity of making the knife. The set has
been included in the catalogue since 1997.

▶ These *Cruets* for oil and vinegar
with counter-weighted lid,
designed in 1980, have become
a quintessential classic of the
Castiglioni style.

▼ The *Dry* service marked our debut in cutlery
manufacture (1982).

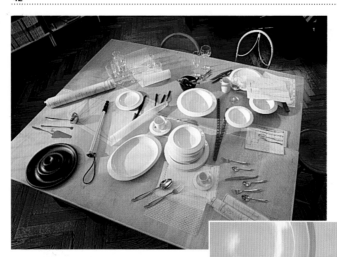

▲ The *Bavero* (1997) porcelain service, displayed here on the workbench, is another superb specimen of Castiglioni's work. This project draws its raison d'être from what the architect refers to as "the principal design element", in other words the key project idea that the designer must seize, the intuition at the start of any job: in this case, it's a simple (but highly significant, not to say bold) design move—folding the edges of the plates downwards.

▲ Such has been the success of *Bavero* that in 2001 we are launching new items for the service, plus a decorated version. Once again, the *à la Castiglioni* treatment is expressed through the simple decision to apply light azure to the folds of certain items in the service.

▲ New for the 2001 *Bavero* service, *Tea for Two*, based upon the simpatico and extremely practical *Cabaré* melamine tray.

▶ Picking up on the theme of *ready-made*, this prototype seven-armed candelabra is called *Menorah*, and rests on the rubber covering of a Japanese motorbike grip. Three of them were produced for the "Nerot Mitzvah, Contemporary ideas for light in the Jewish Ritual" research project, promoted by our common friend Izzika Gaon of the Israel Museum in Jerusalem.

◀ Castiglioni's sense of practicality, his attention to everyday whims, come out in the *Mayonnaise spoon*, conceived specially for scooping up the stuff that sticks to the inside of the jar. This spoon was originally designed with Pier Giacomo as a promotional gadget for Kraft, and manufactured by us in 1997.

ALESSI

Alessandro Mendini

● It is by no means easy to describe Alessandro Mendini's relations with myself and Alessi. What I can say is that for me he has been the master, in a vaguely Socratic fashion, who has gradually introduced me to the many mysteries of our fascinating profession. When people ask me what Mendini does for us, what his role is, I can only smile: Sandro is such a *sui generis* consultant that his position cannot really be described outside its context: a relationship similar to Peter Behrens' with AEG of Rathenau.

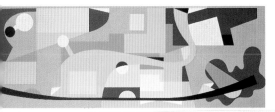

Mendini began working with us in 1977 when, under his guidance, a design and architecture magazine destined to make quite a stir over the following years, *Modo*, first started.

▲ It is Mendini who designed my living space, the "House of Happiness." As well as drawing the plan (above), Alessandro coordinated the work of the other architects involved.

▶ The series of small kitchen electrical tools saw Mendini right in the midst of a joint venture uniting Alessi and Philips, opening up new horizons for international partnerships.

▲ Typical of Mendini's work are the meticulous "maps" in which characters, objects, things and settings are placed in a chain of relations, as in a topographical sequence, in which every step adds to understanding the meaning of the journey.

▶ *Cioccolator*: this calculator does not set out to make math better, its purpose is simply to put the fun back into numerical calculations, to banish the lack of emotional connection in an activity all too often performed with aesthetically and sensorially deficient tools (2000).

ALESSI

▶ Somehow, in an extremely informal way, Mendini is aware of our most intimate problems and wishes… without even meeting up that often; over the years we have perfected a way of working together that is almost telepathic…

A·ALESSI
A·MENDINI

VENTI ANNI DI COLLABORAZIONE

SERVIZIO PIATTI

◀ In 1986 a porcelain plate service designed by Mendini, assisted by Annalisa Margarini, went into production. Alessandro came up with the *How Much White* basic service and the *How Many Stars* version, with delicate gilded ornaments, while the polychrome triangles in the very vivacious *How Many Colours* decoration are by Nicola De Maria.

Author of the research project *Paesaggio casalingo* and other books, Mendini is Alessi's official chronicler. As a designer, he continues to design objects, often in the most complex and moving areas of our catalogue. As an architect, he has designed my home (the "House of Happiness"), two extensions for the factory at Crusinallo, the Alessi museum and the layout of several exhibitions. In his role as design manager he has been responsible for the invention and coordination of some of our most legendary design processes, a few of which are illustrated here. As a consultant, he has brought to my attention a huge number of designers who have gone on to work with us.

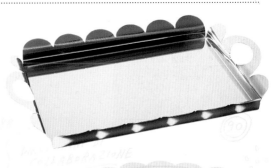

▲ The popular *Recinto* family (born in 1997) of trays and baskets with a scalloped border. It's plain to see that the trays are tremble-proof, thanks to thick handles for a better grip, and a "safety" edge: in profile, they hint at generous giving, the transfer from inside to outside, though not without a hint of self-mockery.

▲ *Anna Set* (2001): this Mendinian interpretation of the central European and Anglo-Saxon creamer and sugar set is a point of cross-over between Alessi's two most famous families: *Anna* and *Recinto*.

▶ A limited edition collection of mosaic *Recinto* trays: a joint project for 2000, with mosaic specialist Bisazza from the Veneto region.

Alessi. Extra ordinary.

▼ The *Anna Cheese* (1999) grater is an interesting departure from all the other graters we make: the grater itself revolves around the piece of cheese. Mendini drew his inspiration from a classic grater made in Savoy, with teeth cut the Italian way, ideal for grating parmesan and other hard cheeses.

▲ The extraordinary success of the corkscrew made it inevitable that the popular *Anna* icon would grow into a small family. Her cult status is wittily underlined in this Lowe Lintas Pirella Göttsche advert, which has her depicted as a new Marilyn for the twenty-first century.

▲ *Anna Box* box (1999).

◀ *Anna Light* lighter (1998).

▶ I'm especially proud of the *Anna G.* corkscrew (1994), which immediately became our top bestseller, thereby debunking the rumour (slyly put about by the man himself) that Mendini only designs objects which don't sell!

▼ *Anna Pepper* peppermill (1998).

▲ *Anna Time* timer (1999).

▲ *Anna Stop* stopper (1999).

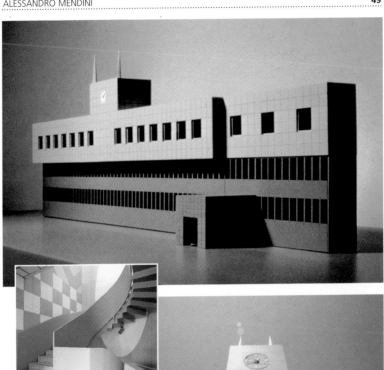

▲ Alessi's Crusinallo
headquarters (1994)
bears the mark of the
Atelier Mendini, with a vital
contribution by Francesco
Mendini: here, the plan for
extension, and the reception
area stairs leading to the
exhibition hall (1995).

◄ The allusive Alessi stand
at the Frankfurt Fair.

▲ The Omegna *Forum*, the new museum of local arts and traditions (1998), designed by the Atelier Mendini.

◄ The conference room at Alessi's Hamburg offices, a Mendini design too, with the reassuring shapes of the *100% Make Up* vases (1996).

► The interior of the first Macef stand, with its characteristic revolving display area.

Tea & Coffee Piazza

▲ Robert Venturi's objects, marked by their subtle decoration, are set on a tray reproducing Piazza Campidoglio.

● In 1979 Alessandro Mendini's exuberant mind came up with the idea of setting "pure" architects the task of designing an object, the classic tea and coffee service. Produced in a run of ninety-nine each, the eleven silver services came out with the Officina Alessi brand and the designer's monogram. In 1983 they were presented to the public in an exhibition arranged by Hans Hollein at the San Carpoforo church in Milan.

▲ Japanese logic and precision for Kazumasa Yamashita: the knobs of these recipients form the initials of their contents.

◄ Ironic and eclectic postmodern for Charles Jencks, who designs extravagant tubby columns with capitals, somewhere between surprise and parody.

▶ With this project Aldo Rossi demonstrates his talents as a designer: the tray turns into a home tabernacle to officiate the hospitable rite of coffee.

▼ Paolo Portoghesi uses hexagons and pyramids to sculpt a domestic citadel for those little pleasures, even—the only designer to do so—adding an ash-tray for smokers.

▼ It's all curves in Alessandro Mendini's design, which seems to breathe new life into the timeless *Bombé*: the articles are ready to leap from their slender pedestals.

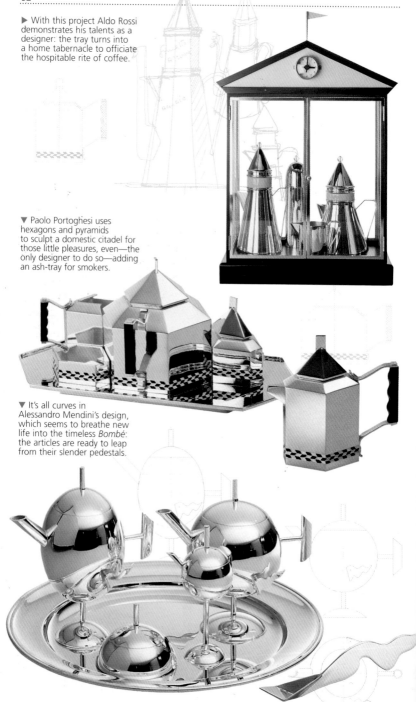

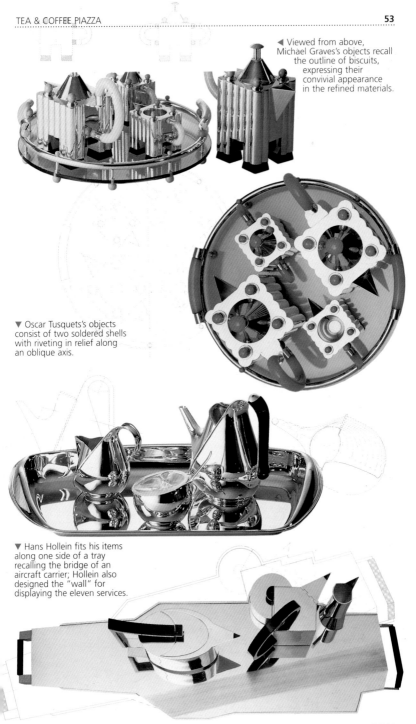

◄ Viewed from above, Michael Graves's objects recall the outline of biscuits, expressing their convivial appearance in the refined materials.

▼ Oscar Tusquets's objects consist of two soldered shells with riveting in relief along an oblique axis.

▼ Hans Hollein fits his items along one side of a tray recalling the bridge of an aircraft carrier; Hollein also designed the "wall" for displaying the eleven services.

ALESSI

▼ Eerie little hands poke out of Stanley Tigerman's tray, while the spouts are shaped as inviting half-open lips (a detail requiring a high-risk technical approach).

The *Tea & Coffee Piazza* series takes up and develops two major themes: the concept of "artistic multiple" and the involvement of international architects in the quest for design. This feature was strongly promoted by Mendini, who foretold the end of "Bel design italiano" and, setting himself "at the crossroads between awareness of tradition and the lure of the unknown", felt the need to go back to the roots of the phenomenon of design,

to the fifties, when "pure" architects began to design objects. Indeed, not only did this venture start off the trend of highly expressive, postmodern "objects of emotion" *style symbol*, it enabled me to make an incredible number of contacts and have new experiences which would come in very handy for the product policy of the following years. As a research venture, we owe it the discovery of two great new designers: Aldo Rossi and Michael Graves.

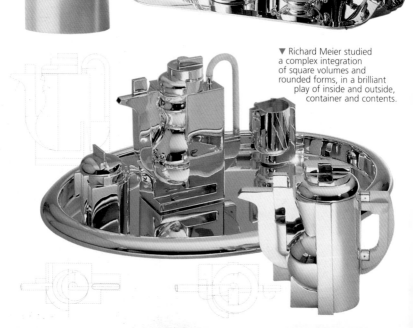

▼ Richard Meier studied a complex integration of square volumes and rounded forms, in a brilliant play of inside and outside, container and contents.

Aldo Rossi

● Aldo Rossi was a lake-lover like me. He was never happier than when he went to meditate and write at the old family house on Lake Mergozzo, I found out when we first met in the spring of 1980. He designed some of the most representative of our eighties articles, and had an ability—which only the great designers have—to tune in to the public mood. Rossi regarded design as something of a hobby; his first love was always architecture. He died in an accident on Lake Maggiore. The first of my masters to pass away. I miss him terribly, I'm very sad to say.

❝ *I feel there is often something mysterious in the process of selling objects: sometimes I see objects as clay relics ranged in museums; a material enclosing a world that perhaps merely desires to be used and destroyed. There are always two ways of looking at things…* **❞**

▶ The *Momento* range of watches (1987) is the only one still in the Alessi catalogue. Aldo loved watches and clocks, often incorporating them into his public buildings.

◀ Rossi's dream was to produce a new Moka to sell to all, if possible at a low price: he got very close with his *La cupola* aluminium espresso coffee maker (1988).

ALESSI

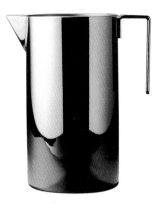

◄ Throughout August 1997 I kept the prototype of his *Pitcher* in my car: I knew that Aldo was due to come to Lake Maggiore, and he would have been happy to see it. He never got the chance.

▼ The *Press filter coffee maker* made during the research that resulted in *Cupola* (1986).

As can be seen from the design of a coffee-maker "protected" by *San Carlone* of Arona, Aldo had a way of relating to our engineers that was worlds away from what we had experienced: he made sketches, presented them, and then waited for the engineers to make all their comments and changes, even sweeping ones.
It seemed as if everything was OK! For Uncle and Casalino, fresh from the relationship with Sapper, this was a scandalous attitude. One day Uncle said to him in his grumpy way:
But, really, couldn't you bring us finished designs rather than these sketches which are only half done?
That was the only time I ever saw Rossi get angry. He answered dryly that if we wanted final-draft technical designs, then we could get them from Zanuso, but not from him. Rossi's attitude helped me to understand an approach to design not restricted to himself, but shared to some degree by all or almost all designers who have experience as architects.

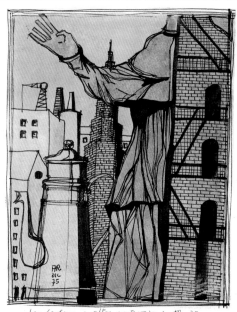

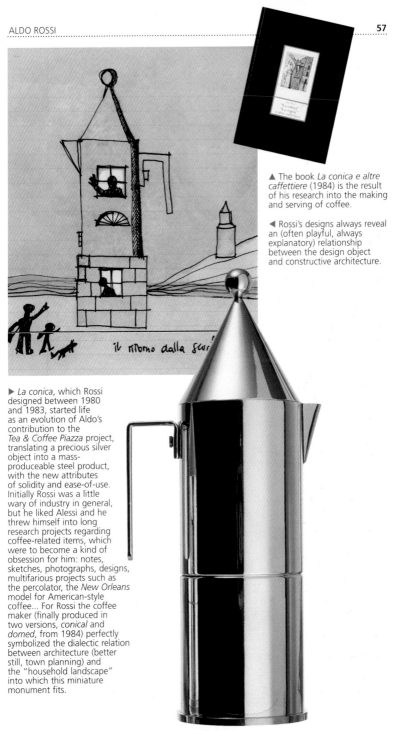

il ritorno dalla scu...

▲ The book *La conica e altre caffettiere* (1984) is the result of his research into the making and serving of coffee.

◄ Rossi's designs always reveal an (often playful, always explanatory) relationship between the design object and constructive architecture.

▶ *La conica*, which Rossi designed between 1980 and 1983, started life as an evolution of Aldo's contribution to the *Tea & Coffee Piazza* project, translating a precious silver object into a mass-produceable steel product, with the new attributes of solidity and ease-of-use. Initially Rossi was a little wary of industry in general, but he liked Alessi and he threw himself into long research projects regarding coffee-related items, which were to become a kind of obsession for him: notes, sketches, photographs, designs, multifarious projects such as the percolator, the *New Orleans* model for American-style coffee... For Rossi the coffee maker (finally produced in two versions, *conical* and *domed*, from 1984) perfectly symbolized the dialectic relation between architecture (better still, town planning) and the "household landscape" into which this miniature monument fits.

ALESSI

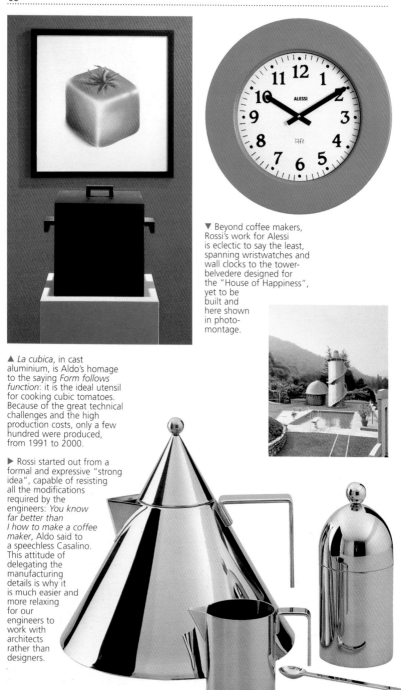

▼ Beyond coffee makers, Rossi's work for Alessi is eclectic to say the least, spanning wristwatches and wall clocks to the tower-belvedere designed for the "House of Happiness", yet to be built and here shown in photo-montage.

▲ *La cubica*, in cast aluminium, is Aldo's homage to the saying *Form follows function*: it is the ideal utensil for cooking cubic tomatoes. Because of the great technical challenges and the high production costs, only a few hundred were produced, from 1991 to 2000.

▶ Rossi started out from a formal and expressive "strong idea", capable of resisting all the modifications required by the engineers: *You know far better than I how to make a coffee maker*, Aldo said to a speechless Casalino. This attitude of delegating the manufacturing details is why it is much easier and more relaxing for our engineers to work with architects rather than designers.

In the days of the "famous" clash over technical drawings, my uncle was bewildered, but at the next opportunity he managed to redeem himself by comparing Aldo's designs to those of Morandi. Aldo was struck, and from that moment a great passion grew between the two of them, culminating in the design for my cousin Stefano's house at Suna (1995).

Michael Graves

“ *With Alessi, tradition extends to the idea of family. As a designer you and your people are brought in and treated as member of a family–it's a very personal relationship of designer and manufacturer. This is what ties everything.* ”

● As far back as January 1980, during our first visit to his big studio in Princeton, Michael Graves told us that from then on he would be spending at least half his time on design. It was a definitive statement, one which corresponded to his great potential. He has an incredible ability to tune in to public taste, even that of the man on the street: he is not a lover of theory, but he once admitted his wish to help create an "American style".

▶ The 1985 *Kettle with bird* continues to go from strength to strength. It spawned a "family" of objects which Graves dauntlessly continues to expand, year after year, developing his own sensitivity towards a less intellectualized approach to design, softer than its European equivalents.

Graves' highly personal and easy to recognize formal style blends influences from the European tradition, Art Deco, American "pop", and flashes of pre-Columbian culture. He has shown he can bewitch the public like only very few of the designers with whom I've worked. I think that his success derives from his wholly uninhibited approach to the economic dimension which this activity inevitably entails, an attitude that enables him to read the expectations of the public more clearly than his European counterparts.

▶ The articles in the "Graves family" came to life concentrically, developing around the *Kettle*, which was initially joined by the *Cream jug*, the *Sugar bowl* (1988) and the big two-litre *Carafe* (1991). Reinforcements arrived in the shape of *Pelican* (1995), the espresso coffee maker.

▼ This *Kitchen oil cruet* (1999) is a recent example of Graves in his finest pop mode.

▲ The designs in the background are from sketches for the service he made as part of the *Tea & Coffee Piazza* project, the first time Graves and Alessi worked together.

ALESSI

▶ The original *Photo holder* in steel and thermoplastic resin (1997).

▶ In the eighties, Michael Graves' collections paved the way for multiple colours in the domestic environment; to this day, they remain typical of our taste for tonal colours. From 2000 on the colour panorama is enhanced by a new set of surface finishes, working with the material qualities of metallic surfaces, to offer fresh interpretations of objects in our back-catalogue.

◀ *Corkscrew, Champagne cap, Pepper mill, Salt castor* and *Kitchen timer*: for Graves the concept of "family" spans a horizon of different items, every year increasing in extent, right down to the tiniest of pieces.

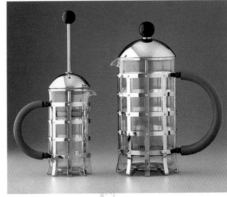

▲ *Demitasse cup, Mug, Butter dish* and *Press filter coffee maker*: an unmistakable look for objects well shielded by rings of steel, with easy-grip handles, ideal for those drowsy, half-asleep breakfasts (1989).

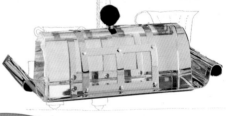

◀ Polyamide handles make a comeback in this indispensable *Tray* (1994).

ALESSI

◀ The *Bread bin* (1997) takes us back to a special spot in Graves's memory: the paunchy recipient is replete with nostalgia for the breakfast American children used to eat before the ready-made snack age, when it was an indispensable treasure chest guarding the aroma of freshly baked bread.

▼ The delicate colour combination of yellow and blue sets off one of Graves' two *Porcelain services* (1994–99).

▲ The slim *Pepper mill* (1993) is one of the *Twergi* objects.

▶ The *Cheese board* rests on a broad steel tray, and is made up of a ceramic cutting board "with holes", crowned by a transparent cover: the handle is a smiling mouse. Available in a range of colours, as is the *Bread bin* above.

▼ The *Kitchen clock* is the missing link between the "birdie" family (the bird is on the hands) and the bright colours of the *Euclid* series (1992).

▲ As well as his wooden objects for *Twergi*, Graves miniaturized architecture for this *Mantel clock*, with the clock face on the "piano nobile" of an edifice supported by squat columns (1988–99).

▼ With its characteristic shape *Medium vase* (1997) looks a little like a porcelain rendition of cut bamboo, a paradoxical and worthy citation of vases made in Malaysia, the only country in the world not to use ceramics.

▼ In his most recent work for Alessi, Graves has focused on porcelain, transferring typically architectural motifs to objects which could be considered the "skyscrapers".

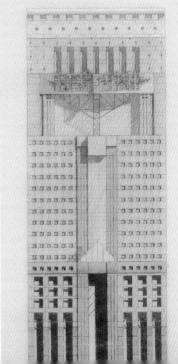

Other Designers

● I have worked with hundreds of designers since the early seventies. This has been the most rewarding experience of my life, and I continue to be thrilled by it. I am a lucky man: each of these encounters has left me with something of importance. I love seeing how, each time, the vastness of the Creative Possible gels into images, words, gestures and thoughts, always unique, yet always focused on the heroic exploit of expressing something that is larger than we are. I am yet to understand the mysterious way that some of these designers have built up families in our catalogue, while many others have seemingly left a more fleeting trace… But what I do know is that just one project is all it takes to add something to this great game of life.

▲ *The Soundtrack* is a new departure for Alessi: a self-adhesive compact disc holder in thermoplastic resin. The decoration is designed by Javier Mariscal. I had been working for many years with Ron, without finding anything for a production run, until one evening in the spring of 1997 he called me, saying he had a great project for me, that he would fax it to me right away. How thrilling! After so many years, for the first time I had before me a concrete example of what I call *Less is more*, the personification of the prophecy of immaterial design for the next century, the absence of an authoritative personal style. And what class! *The Soundtrack* is one of the most brilliant projects I have come across in at least ten years.

◀ *Babyboop* (2000) is the first design Ron has made for us in steel. It's a set of three small containers for nibbles, shaped to reflect the large blow-molded aluminium furniture/sculptures he made in a limited run in the late 90s.

Riccardo Dalisi

▶ His research into the *Neapolitan coffee maker* (1979–87, winning the XIIth Compasso d'Oro) was the longest in our history: over the years it led to one book and over two hundred fully working prototypes in tin. Wearing a beret and clothes straight out of a neo-realist film, continuously turning over new ideas and trying out new ways of making things work, Dalisi has not been an easy person to manage, but this was a very important project for us indeed. It enabled us to open up our manufacturing world even more to the conceptual experience of the artisan; it taught us to dilute our certainties in a fragile and poetic light, which is so necessary to work on extremely deep-rooted household rituals.

Andrea Branzi

« Building a house for somebody means building a place and objects with which one can enter in relations, not just of use and functionality, but also psychological, symbolic and poetic. Holderlin used to say Man lives poetically, *which means that the relations that link a person to his nest are literary in nature—partly obscure—and symbolic. »*

▼ A designer who requires the public at large to meet him halfway, as Branzi himself will not deny, but what can you say when a simple *Solferino* (2000) openwork citrus holder such as this encapsulates the finest twentieth-century contemporary art has to offer?

◀ *Mama-ò*, Branzi's kettle designed in 1988, has two symmetrical spouts with a melodic whistle, connected by a long handle.

▼ Concerned about ecology and natural forms, Branzi is one of the designers most sensitive to the turned wood of *Twergi*. His family, recognizable by their lengthened, linked lozenge decoration also includes the witty *Toothpick holder* (1991) and the *Bottle-opener* (1999).

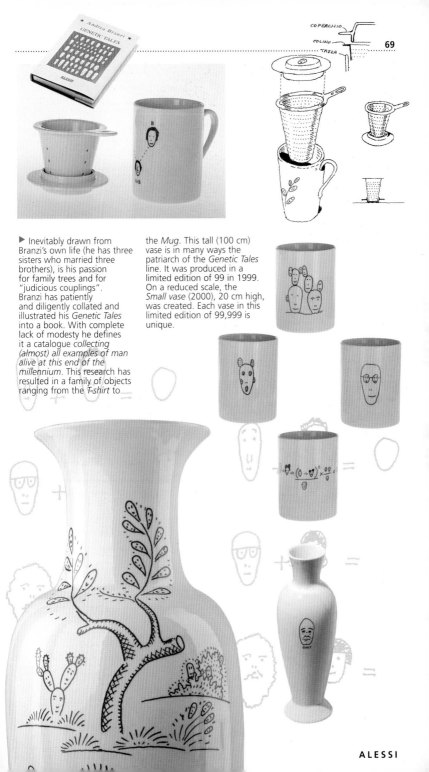

▶ Inevitably drawn from Branzi's own life (he has three sisters who married three brothers), is his passion for family trees and for "judicious couplings". Branzi has patiently and diligently collated and illustrated his *Genetic Tales* into a book. With complete lack of modesty he defines it a catalogue *collecting (almost) all examples of man alive at this end of the millennium*. This research has resulted in a family of objects ranging from the *T-shirt* to the *Mug*. This tall (100 cm) vase is in many ways the patriarch of the *Genetic Tales* line. It was produced in a limited edition of 99 in 1999. On a reduced scale, the *Small vase* (2000), 20 cm high, was created. Each vase in this limited edition of 99,999 is unique.

Norman Foster

▶ With this rectangular colour aluminium *Tray* (1998), Foster returns to the essential, streamlined simplicity of certain Japanese objects, such as the low-slung futon. This simplicity in everyday gestures (handing things out, or sleeping) is reflected in the extremely subtle curve, which lends a relaxing gentleness to the tray silhouette.
Rack (2000) is an indispensable accessory for wall-hanging this outsize tray.

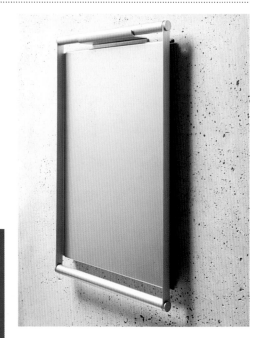

Paolo Portoghesi

◀ The interwoven chapel arches of Achphat in Armenia and the subtle lines of the Tlemcen mosque in North Africa have inspired this micro-architecture, where Portoghesi's trademark bundle of lines culminates in the magical light of a candle (1988–98).

Lluís Clotet

▼ Captivated by the whimsical crumpled effect of a silver paper tray, Clotet reproduced the effect in stainless steel (1994).

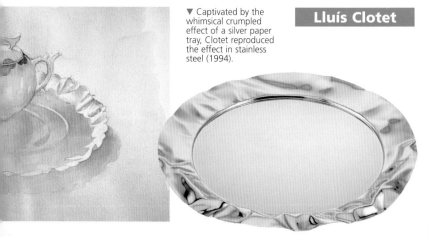

Frank Gehry

▼ *Pito* is the kettle designed by Gehry, with a mahogany handle and melodic stopper.

« When the artists and sculptors I know are working, there is always an element of play involved. They experiment, try things out. A slightly naïve and infantile way of doing things, like children playing in a sandbox. Scientists work in a similar way. It's like casting away baggage until one is free to follow ideas, rather than seeking to see where one is headed. »

Mario Botta

◄ "No preciousness, no pedantic pernicketiness, no evident sophistry: Botta's style is modest, balanced, and never convoluted." (F. Chaslin, 1982) *Mia* and *Tua* (2000) are two large carafes for water and wine—the first Alessi household project by this Swiss architect since his *Eye* watch (1989–97).

ALESSI

Jasper Morrison

● What I like about Morrison is the courage and modesty he brings to his life as a designer. He knows only too well that in our field major innovation hardly ever comes about from great leaps forward, but rather it is the result of small and progressive improvements, dominated by the rich and fertile terrain of ancient ritual.

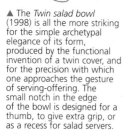

▲ *Socrates* is a corkscrew (1998): the philosopher's maieutics strike again, providing expression of the ideas within the person/object with whom you have a dialogue.

▲ The *Twin salad bowl* (1998) is all the more striking for the simple archetypal elegance of its form, produced by the functional invention of a twin cover, and for the precision with which one approaches the gesture of serving-offering. The small notch in the edge of the bowl is designed for a thumb, to give extra grip, or as a recess for salad servers.

▶ Casbah, sweet casbah... *Pepe le Moko* (1998) grinds sea salt and various types of peppercorns.

▼ Interactivity, solutions for two objects which can be brought together: *Op* is a tray; *Op-la* turns into a table-tray with a stainless steel base (1998).

▲ *Tin family* (1998) is a family of stainless steel containers for storing salt, sugar, cereals, biscuits and cakes. Morrison takes the history of design types forwards once more, cautiously and bravely taking small but crucial steps.

◀ For many years I was on the lookout for a good contemporary design for a new serving dish that not only met all professional catering standards, but had a design that made it suited to home use too. I personally find that there is no better serving dish than a nice big stainless steel plate—resilient, indestructible, extremely hygienic and easy to clean. Finally, in 2000, it happened. In a moment of grace, with the assistance of gastronome Alberto Gozzi, Jasper succeeded where so many other designers have failed: a three dimensional serving dish, in the most classic old Sheffield tradition, revisited!

ALESSI

Massimo Morozzi

◄ *Pasta set* is, simply, a homage to pasta. Morozzi showed me the project in 1982. The shape of the object was attractive and yet mysterious. We organized a survey: roughly half of those interviewed did not realize it was a saucepan for boiling water, and came up with all kinds of interpretations. Nevertheless, we decided to manufacture it, and that was a sound decision. *Pasta set* has become so popular that it has had a profound influence on the market, winning the Gold Medal in 1986 at the Ljubljana Bio 11, and spawning at least a hundred imitators the world over. The project continued with *Vapor set* (1990) designed for steam cooking.

Fig. 13

Abdi Abdelkader

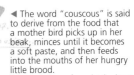

◀ The word "couscous" is said to derive from the food that a mother bird picks up in her beak, minces until it becomes a soft paste, and then feeds into the mouths of her hungry little brood.

It is a mixture of crushed wheat, millet or rice flour, steamed and usually eaten with chicken or mutton and various pulses. This delicious dish has long been a ritual offering in Mediterranean African countries; it is also one of the most widely eaten dishes in the world. Continuing with our range of utensils for ethnic cuisines, we commissioned Abdi Abdelkader of Algeria to design this *Couscoussière*, along with the *Gsâa* large ceramic container and the *Container* for spices (1999).

Alberto Meda

▼ Inspired by the maxim "save energy, stay warm", Meda's *Kalura* hotplate (2001) is an energy-conscious, practical and exceedingly efficient household appliance, designed to minimize electricity use and cut long-term consumption. Just a few minutes after plugging it in, it has accumulated all the energy it needs to keep food warm at the table for an hour. An extremely rare beast, this: a wireless appliance (it comes to the table minus its electricity cable) free from an encumberment common to practically every single household appliance. It is a useful and practical addition to the stage where everyday we play out our convivial moments.

Marc Newson

● I first heard of Marc in the mid-eighties. Massimo Morozzi met Marc on a triumphant trip to Australia, and came back with a prototype of his first wristwatch, which now has a proud place in the Alessi Museum. Massimo told me that Marc was a very young Australian designer destined, in his opinion, to go a long, long way. Born in 1963, Newson certainly has gone a long way, and is one of the most promising young designers at work today.

◀ The *Gemini* salt mill and pepper mill and *Stavros* bottle-opener (1999) are fine examples of what I like about his work: his ability to develop his own style, imbued with great originality; in other words, an aptitude for creating striking objects, characterized by a truly innovative form, despite working within a context such as ours in which everything, or practically everything, has already been designed, manufactured, seen and sold.

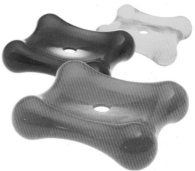

▲ The *Sygma* clothes-rack and *Titan* soap dish (1999). I find his forms are extraordinarily faithful to his ideograms, stylistic approach, or whatever you want to call it, characteristic of the profound figurative culture of his country. His projects allude to the archetypal forms of aborigine artifacts, as well as objects crafted by nature: for example, bowls hollowed out by the waves of the Australian Ocean, or the colours of certain corals, or tree roots polished smooth by millennia of rain. It is this, his way of masterfully depicting some of the typical and fundamental characteristics of his homeland, both in a miraculously new fashion, and through simple repetition and copying, that is the most wonderful compliment I could pay him.

Arnell & Bickford

◀ *Rosenschale* is the critical reconstruction of the prototype of a fruit basket designed by Josef Hoffmann in 1906, and never manufactured. Arnell and Bickford worked solely from a photograph—no sketches or drawings have ever been found.

D'Urbino & Lomazzi

◀ *Augh!* (2000): Paolo Lomazzi and Donato D'Urbino, furniture design pioneers since the 60s, have turned their hands to the extendible trivet.

Oscar Tusquets

▶ The *Hot Sweet Hot* oven thermometer is one of three home thermometers designed by Tusquets and manufactured since 1998. Oscar designed it with input from his wife, Victoria Roqué, a great Spanish cook.

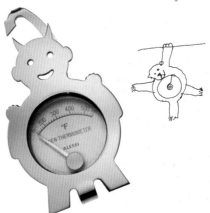

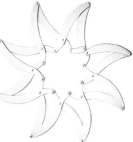

A L E S S I

Wolfgang Hints

▶ I admit it: even though the spiceholder idea has featured a great deal among objects of recent years, I simply couldn't resist the brilliance of Wolfgang Hints's stackable container, *Spice Tower* (2000). Hints is a young designer who served as my assistant at a workshop at the Hochschule für Angewandte Kunst in Vienna in the mid-nineties.

Khodi Feiz

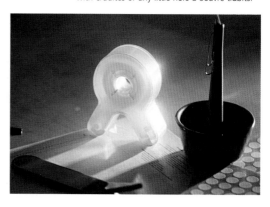

◀ 100% Iranian and not a fundamentalist bone in his body, Khodi Feiz is a real citizen of the world. He has come up with a new departure for us, inspired by gastronomic traditions far removed from his original culture. The *Salsa* container (2000) is ideal not only for serving the Mexican dish from which it takes its name, but also goes divinely with crudités or any little hors d'oeuvre tidbits.

▶ The home or office work desk theme, tackled with Feiz's rather playful touch: the *Quack* adhesive tape dispenser, *Ali-the-gator* paperknife and *Clip-tree* paperclip holder (2001).

Massimo Scolari

◀ Tools to read and write well by... as computer mice run rampant, Scolari (the name aptly means scholars in Italian!) in 1998 comes up with a *Pencil* in ebonized wood with a lead-tin alloy tip, and a *Paperknife-bookmark*, with two page-marking ribbons, specially designed for people who read books whose pages need cutting.

Donata Paruccini

◀ *The Fly* (2001) drawing pins are a metaphorically hyper-realist interpretation of the work desk theme by young designer Paruccini.

George Sowden

▼ To soften the invasive finality of a timer's ring, Sowden designed *Alphonse* (1997), an electronic timer which, when the time is up, plays a little tune composed by Steve Piccolo. Which tune it plays depends on the object's colour.

▲ Sowden's typical soft, rounded contours and lively colours on his eight function desktop calculator, *Dauphine* (1997).

ALESSI

Robert Venturi

« What I love about architecture is its complexity and contradiction. I don't like the incoherence and arbitrary nature of bad architecture, nor the over-elaboration of the picturesque or of expressionism. I love hybrid elements rather than pure ones, the results of compromise rather than cleanliness, the crooked rather than the straight, ambiguity rather than articulation. I prefer richness of meaning to clarity of meaning: I prefer disorder bursting with vitality to obvious single-mindedness: I accept the non sequitur and proclaim duality. But architecture founded on complexity and contradiction requires a special kind of commitment to the whole. It has to pursue the elusive unity of inclusion, as opposed to the facile unity of exclusion. More is not less. »

▼ Part of the *Tea & Coffee Piazza* project, *The Campidoglio* tray (1985) echoes Michelangelo's paving in Rome's Capitol Square, highlighting its exceptional perspective shift between the circle and ellipse.

▲ *Cuckoo clock* (1988–96) is an amusing challenge for Venturi, coming to grips with a popular genre, very different from *Campidoglio*.

Marco Zanuso

▲ The *Duna* range of cutlery (1995) is our sole Zanuso project, though I see him as something of the Daddy of Italian design. This was designed as a submission to the 1960 competition held by the U.S. firm Reed & Burton. I clearly recall him describing the central element of imagination behind these items as the "narrow life", that is the tapering of the end part of the handle, mirroring the dresses of young ladies from well-to-do fifties families.

Philippe Starck

" Alessi sells joy! "

● Starck began working with me in 1986, on the French design project *Projet Solférino*, organized together with the Centre Pompidou and François Burkhardt. I cannot help thinking of Starck as the *designer terrible* of our decade. He is a living example of my dream: design, real design, is always highly charged with innovation towards the world of manufacturing and trade, bringing results that need no longer be justified solely on a technological or balance sheet level. A true work of design must move people, convey feelings, bring back memories, surprise, transgress… it must make us feel, intensely, that we are living our one single life… in sum, it has to be poetic. Design is one of the most apt poetic forms of expression of our day. And I know that this great visionary still has plenty of surprises up his sleeve, despite his threats to retire!

▲ Starck, "hung" on the hooks of his *Faitoo*. Leader of the renaissance in French design, in this brilliant and daring identity photo cum marketing ploy Starck shows he is quick to share the fate of his objects.

◀ A lover of precision instruments (see the *Coo-coo* radio, 1996, right), Starck is also happy to design more commonplace objects, such as this *Dr. Spoon* ear-cleaner, *Dr. Kiss* toothbrush, *Dr. Kleen* toothpick (1998) and *Dr. Cheese* inter-dental brush (1998–99).

◄ The *Hot Bertaa* kettle (1990–97) is skewered by its handle-spout. During the design stage, its compact, almost sacred appearance was shrouded in an aura of mysticism: in his preliminary sketches Starck had penned a Latin inscription around its base.

▶ With the *Boaat* (1998) series, a range of kitchen containers with lids and bowls with feet, Starck continues his research into archetypal eating objects, this time drawing inspiration from Japanese cuisine.

ALESSI

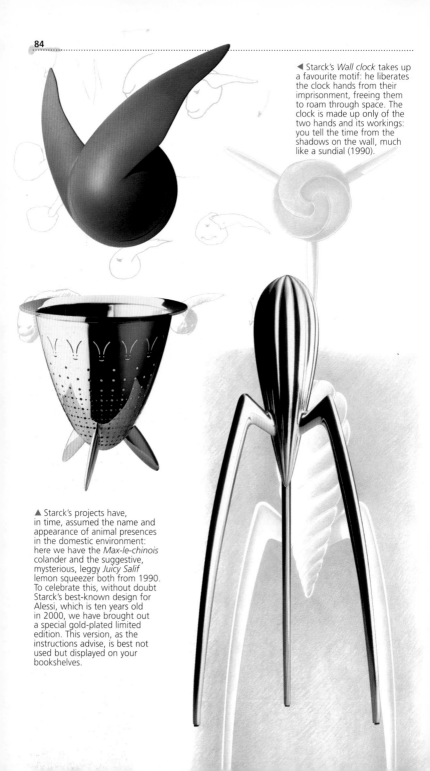

◀ Starck's *Wall clock* takes up a favourite motif: he liberates the clock hands from their imprisonment, freeing them to roam through space. The clock is made up only of the two hands and its workings: you tell the time from the shadows on the wall, much like a sundial (1990).

▲ Starck's projects have, in time, assumed the name and appearance of animal presences in the domestic environment: here we have the *Max-le-chinois* colander and the suggestive, mysterious, leggy *Juicy Salif* lemon squeezer both from 1990. To celebrate this, without doubt Starck's best-known design for Alessi, which is ten years old in 2000, we have brought out a special gold-plated limited edition. This version, as the instructions advise, is best not used but displayed on your bookshelves.

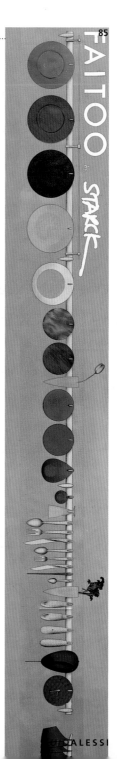

▲ *Faitoo*, "fait-tout", came out in 1996. In French it means both "do-it-all" and saucepan. It is a long bar to hang in the kitchen, with hooks for hanging all kinds of things by their handles or through special holes. Everything is visible and within reach, spelling an end to those frustrating "where can it be?" moments in the kitchen.

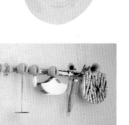

▲ *Voilà Voilà*: the tray rushes along on its little green feet (1992).

▲ The *Cake server* looks as solid and manoeuvrable as a bricklayer's trowel (1998).

▲ The unmistakable silhouette of *Mister Meumeu* conceals a parmesan cheese cellar with grater: the horn is, in actual fact, a spoon (1992).

▼ The gleaming surface of the *Centre-piece* is supported by "attendants": barely sketched grey or strange characters redolent of Starck's recent "anthropomorphic" works (1996).

◀ Starck's output spans precision mechanisms (such as the clocks or the radio) and seemingly everyday objects, such as the *Dr. Skud* fly swatter which, when moved, reveals a human face (1998).

WELCOME

▲ In 1996 we acquired the small Starck and Patricia company, adding several articles to our catalogue including the *O'Kelvin* candle-stick (1989), *Joe Cactus* ash-tray (1990) and *Berta Youssouf* place-holder (1987).

OFFICINA ALESSI

Dédé
design Philippe Starck, (1994) 1996

▲ The chubby, solitary *Dedé* mediates on his soft aluminium rotundities and on his role as a doorstop (1996).

ALESSI

Enzo Mari

<< Italian design manufacturers are, in actual fact, metaphors for manufacturers. >>

● Enzo Mari harbours a critical attitude towards our company, despite the fact that it is different from the many others on the international design scene. Without question he is my "master of paranoia": a sort of guardian angel on my shoulder who wags a disapproving finger when I do something he feels I shouldn't! We met in the late seventies, when I wanted to include his *Arran* tray, designed for Danese, in our *Programme 7*—and I succeeded, finally, twenty years later, in 1997. In a conference held in Paris, with his characteristic verbal vehemence, he expressed the concept I have cited above. The words struck me, I made them mine, and the phrase has served as a launchpad for theoretical research into the "Factory of Italian Design". I am delighted he is still working and building up his family in our catalogue. I find his criticisms valuable, every now and then we need him to reset the needle of our compass to North, the direction it should be pointing in, even in mid-storm.

▲ *Ecolo* is Mari's most emblematic project: turning discarded plastic bottles into vases for flowers (1996).

ENZO MARI

▶ Mari has a green thumb, and many of his projects have a strong ecological connotation. The main reason why he created his *Gardening set* for balconies and allotments was probably for his own passion: it includes a stainless steel and aluminium *Trowel* and a pair of dual-purpose tools: a *Trowel/ress* and a *Rake/repotter* (1999).

▲ The *Arran* (1961) rectangular tray, originally designed for Danese, became one of the most significant Italian design projects of the sixties, as well as an archetype in the history of this object. It has been on our catalogue since 1997.

▶ The *Standard* two-level three-wheeled trolley (1989) was Mari's first Alessi project. Designed to be one of the furnishing accessories for my "House of Happiness", it is extremely solid and manoeuvrable: features that make it suited to professional as well as home use.

ALESSI

▶ To my mind, Mari is the greatest proponent of the "stripped-down" approach to design applied to industrial manufacturing: he refrains from the temptations of allowing his fantasy to run wild, so no gratuitous frills creep into his designs just to please the public (he refers to them as *cazzettini*, polite translation of which approximates to "rubbish"). His is just a constant quest for the archetypal simplicity that, on its own, should spawn the birth of a new object into our already overcrowded consumer society. An example is this citrus press (stoically named *Titanic*), in which he inventively tackles and succeeds with all those minor details that have made previous citrus presses unpleasant and sometimes impractical. Not just lovely to look at, it's lightweight and hard-wearing, highly practical, easy and fun to use—in sum, a little masterpiece in its own right, even though its subtlety has sometimes meant that it has had a hard time standing out in the bewildering and crowded landscape of household products…

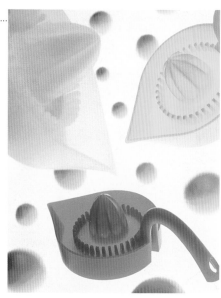

▼ Mari's work at Alessi also includes re-interpreting now "classic" items in new materials: a perfect example is the *Wire basket*, one of the pillars of our company's expansion into steel, this time reinvented in plastic (1997).

▶ The *Kitchen box for salt etc.*, made out of translucent plastic, takes up the sometimes sticky hinge, a popular element in many sixties designs. This interpretation comes up with a brilliant design innovation— the box and lid hook together without needing any intermediate element (1999).

◀ The so-called Mari family of *Strainers and Colanders* (1997), now available in new colours.

▼ Reproductions of several classic Mari designs for Danese from the fifties and sixties. We acquired the rights and put them back into production in 1997.

Twergi and Tendentse

Twergi

● The other deep-rooted manufacturing tradition in the Strona valley, apart from metals, is small wooden items for home and kitchen. In our desire to return to these manufacturing roots, in 1988 we took over the valley's oldest original firm, Battista Piazza 1865. We have reproduced a number of historical items from the first few decades of this century, and revitalized the working of wood: our own designers and many young people have come up with a host of projects using many kinds of wood.

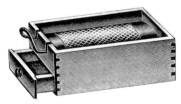

▲ The output of the Piazza firm was an industrial evolution of local crafts. The little elf, known as "twergi" in the Walser dialect, is the historic symbol of this. The good-natured little woodland sprite has been redesigned by Milton Glaser, who has set him on a tiny pair of skis.

▲ Dalisi's pointed *Grinder* (1990–97)) keeps an eye on Michael Graves's pearwood *Tray*; Graves also made the slim *Pepper mill* (1993).

◀ These pages contain the "historical" utensils made by Ubaldo Piazza in the thirties, interspersed with contemporary objects.

▶ The *Mirror* by Ico Migliore and Mara Servetto (1992–98) shyly withdraws before Milton Glaser's *Lamp* (1989–97): looking on are *Photo holders* by Kuno Prey (1990).

▼ Ettore Sottsass fell in love with the *Twergi* wood: all the table articles below are his (1989).

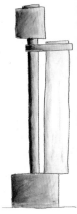

▲ The twin *Portrait holders* (1992–98), inspired by cartoons, bear Guido Venturini's unmistakable touch. The placid cherry wood *Newspaper holder* (1992–98) is by Ico Migliore and Mara Servetto. The steel and wooden *Trolley* (opposite) is by Adalberto Pironi (1996), and doubles as a TV stand. Below, the range of articles designed with a pinch of irreverence by Andrea Branzi, with lozenge decorations (1991). These designs are some of the projects developed by Sottsass, attentive as ever to all aspects of life at the table, right down to the tiniest pieces such as *Egg cups*, *Bottle tops* and *Napkin rings*.

● Tendentse was set up in Livorno to manufacture small articles, principally experimenting with new departures in majolica and porcelain. The first collection included works by Branzi, Cibic, De Lucchi, Gili, Mendini, Morozzi, Mutoh, Nannetti, Nardi, Natalini, Puppa, Raggi, Shama and Tarshito and Sottsass, today all out of production. Since 1989 Tendentse has been part of Alessi.

Tendentse

100% Make Up

● The metaproject of this venture, overseen by Alessandro Mendini, is the production of an ideal aesthetic factory, understood as a multiplication of individuals, as a sequence of aesthetic creatures all resembling one another. To obtain difference from the identical, one hundred authors worked on a single starting shape: in 1992 each finished article was produced in a run of 100, numbered from 1 to 10,000 and signed by all the designers at the same time.

❝ The decorations are like fishes in the sea: they exist even if you can't see them. ❞

▲ Mendini designed the standard gold-coloured vase (number 58 in the series), as well as various other possible decorations and stagings of the hundred vases, drawing ironic inspiration from various sequences or display possibilities.

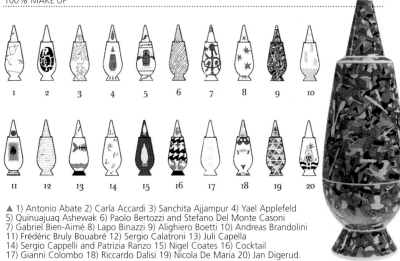

▲ 1) Antonio Abate 2) Carla Accardi 3) Sanchita Ajjampur 4) Yael Applefeld
5) Quinuajuaq Ashewak 6) Paolo Bertozzi and Stefano Del Monte Casoni
7) Gabriel Bien-Aimé 8) Lapo Binazzi 9) Alighiero Boetti 10) Andreas Brandolini
11) Frédéric Bruly Bouabré 12) Sergio Calatroni 13) Juli Capella
14) Sergio Cappelli and Patrizia Ranzo 15) Nigel Coates 16) Cocktail
17) Gianni Colombo 18) Riccardo Dalisi 19) Nicola De Maria 20) Jan Digerud.

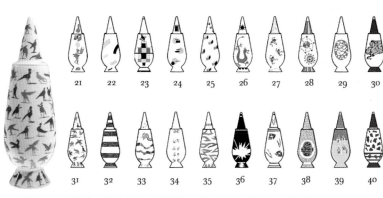

▲ 21) Emmanuel Ekefrey 22) Brian Eno 23) Ellinor Flor 24) Dan Friedman 25) Elizabeth Fritsch
26) Piero Gaeta 27) Giorgio Galli and Beatrice Santiccioli 28) Louise Gibb 29) Piero Gilardi
30) Anna Gili 31) Milton Glaser 32) Michael Graves 33) Maria Christina Hamel
34) Jan Mohamed Hanif 35) Pitt Heinke 36) Yoshiki Hishinuma 37) Susan Holm
38) Yong Ping Huang 39) Aussi Jaffari 40) Christer Jonson.

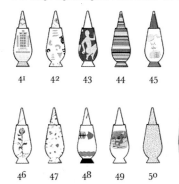

◀ 41) Bodys Isek Kingelez
42) Inka Kivalo
43) Mark Kostabi
44) Randi Kristensen
45) Milan Kunc
46) Kunstflug
47) Shiro Kuramata
48) Quim Larrea
49) Cheikh Ledy
50) Stefan Lindfors.

ALESSI

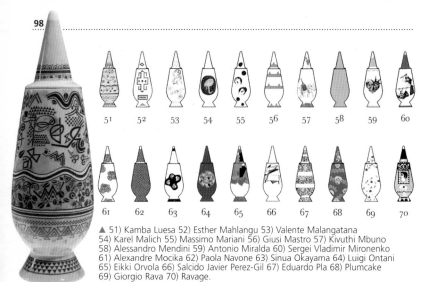

▲ 51) Kamba Luesa 52) Esther Mahlangu 53) Valente Malangatana
54) Karel Malich 55) Massimo Mariani 56) Giusi Mastro 57) Kivuthi Mbuno
58) Alessandro Mendini 59) Antonio Miralda 60) Sergei Vladimir Mironenko
61) Alexandre Mocika 62) Paola Navone 63) Sinua Okayama 64) Luigi Ontani
65) Eikki Orvola 66) Salcido Javier Perez-Gil 67) Eduardo Pla 68) Plumcake
69) Giorgio Rava 70) Ravage.

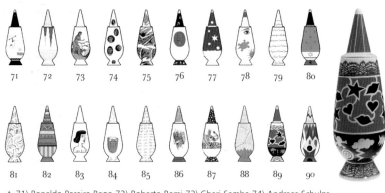

▲ 71) Ronaldo Pereira Rego 72) Roberto Remi 73) Cheri Samba 74) Andreas Schulze
75) Suresh Sethi 76) Raja Babu Sharma 77) Jari Silvennoinen 78) Ettore Sottsass, Jr.
79) Gregorio Spini 80) Philippe Starck 81) Peter Struycken 82) Sybilla 83) Guillermo Tejeda
84) Cyprien Tokoudagba 85) Dagmar Trinks 86) Maurizio Turchet 87) Twins Seven Seven
88) Masanori Umeda 89) Hilde Vemren 90) Robert Venturi.

► 91) Guido
Venturini
92) Nanda Vigo
93) Mara Voce
94) Acharya Vyakul
95) Brigitta Watz
96) Gisbert Weiss
97) Hannes
Wettstein
98) Y.A. Y.A.
Young Aspirations
Young Artists
99) Leonid Yentus
100) Rhonda
Zwillinger.

King-Kong Family

ALESSI

> *We've had enough of erudite designers like Mendini or Branzi, you need to have a degree in architecture to understand their designs... we'd like to design things that appeal to Leo Castelli and to ordinary folk too.*

● In the late eighties, in his usual discreet manner Alessandro Mendini—an invaluable conduit of new talent—told me of two young architects from Florence. Stefano Giovannoni and Guido Venturini came to see me, very nervous, with a few sketches. They were two rather odd looking guys, and I felt that their playful and elementary poetics, often closely inspired by the formal style of cartoons, was full of potential. I had them shown around the factory and did my best to fill them in about us, our hopes and possibilities. They listened to me very attentively, and the next time they came back with a whole book crammed with design notes.

▶ Among their drawings I found a very straightforward tray, its edge perforated with a little man motif, like the ones children cut out with scissors. The *Girotondo* project (1989) went ahead without any particular hitches or special enthusiasm: nobody could have imagined this would become our best-selling tray!

Those little King-Kong "men" have turned up on the edging of objects that belong to the most consolidated Alessi tradition, and therefore seem "normal" to us, such as our *Trays* or *Baskets*. Now, though, they have multiplied and set out to invade territories familiar (such as the chopping board, napkin holder or photo holder) and unfamiliar (keyring, bookmark, candles). Their apotheosis, though, has to be the *Girotondo* Ring-around-the-rosy Jewellery (1998).

To be honest, I think that the King-Kongs, despite their indubitable intuition and great flair, have been lucky too. They were spot on with the "playful style", they understood how important it is to work with "emotional codes", but above all the project came at the right time, and its place in the Alessi catalogue hit the spot.

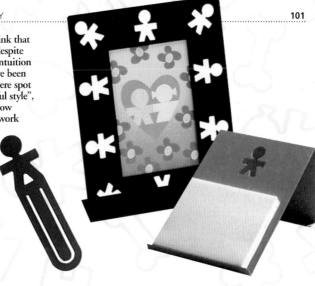

With hindsight, I'd say it was a typical case of applying the "child code" to a catalogue like ours, until then dominated by the authority, status and *style* of great designer's masterpieces: a counterweight to the then emerging talents of Rossi, Graves and Starck.

▶ Alongside the expanding family of "little men", since 1994 we have also seen a range of *Baskets*, *Fruit bowls*, *Trays* and *Breadstick holders* of varying sizes, all perforated with a triangle and rhomboid motif.

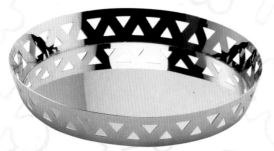

ALESSI

CSA and Young Designers

LAURA

● The Alessi Research Centre (CSA) was set up in 1990 for two purposes: to draw up theoretical papers on topics associated with objects (to be published as books), and to coordinate work with young designers. Up until that time Alessi had only worked with "major designers", and I felt a certain degree of responsibility towards young, upcoming designers. Laura Polinoro, whom Mendini suggested, has done sterling work.

❝ It is not easy to describe this 'workshop': fertile, subtle, a place where, like in a fairytale everything seems possible, where you cannot see a beginning nor know how it will all end...❞

▶ The pictures on this page are taken from a workshop held at the Helsinki University of Industrial and Applied Art in 1996 and in Tokyo in 1997.

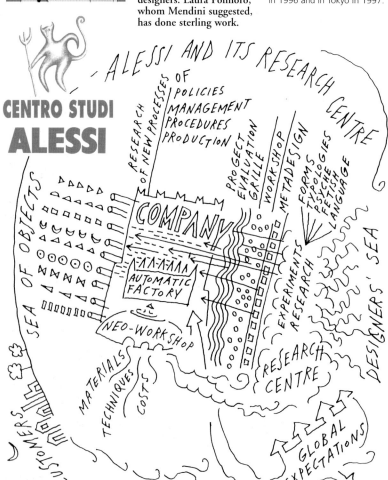

Laura has brought
to Alessi the intuition
and semiological training
garnered at the school
of Eco and Fabbri.
She sometimes reminds
me of Marianne Brandt,
the first woman to work
at the Bauhaus
Metallwerkstatt during
the twenties.
Laura started the arduous
process of shaking Alessi
out of its contentedness
with a certain type of
high-flown Italian design.
Through her we have
brought new disciplines to
bear at Alessi, anthropology
and semiology to name
but two. Nine years on,
in 1998 the CSA of Milan
moved to Crusinallo.

◀ The CSA's design
management work takes
place principally through
workshops and design
seminars with students, in
collaboration with architecture
faculties and schools of art
and design, as well as with
groups of specially invited
designers. We have held
workshops all over the world:
in Argentina, England, Japan,
Brazil, Costa Rica, the U.S.,
Australia, France, Germany,
Finland, Austria, even in the
Aegean Islands.

In 1990 I too was seconded to this task, one which I undertake with great enthusiasm: these photographs show the workshop held at Miami University in 1996.
Each year I do my best to set aside at least two periods to hold personal workshops. I have taken great pleasure in trying to teach young people about my field, and I'm curious to find out what they think about us, how they consider what Alessi is doing. The workshops are not just about teaching, they also play a significant operational role, sometimes leading to veritable projects, or else verifying the suitability of designs for manufacture. To sum up, it's a very interesting part of Alessi's open policy towards the concept of "metaproject", the creation of a structure of ongoing mental research.

▶ Opposite, Christian Jurke's design
(the *Crisute II* electric kettle) developed during
the workshop led by Andreas Brandolini
at the Hochschule der Bildenden Künste,
Saarbrücken (1994–95).

◀ These three photographs, moving top
to bottom, refer to Sebastian Liedtke's *Jelly*
chiller/serving bowl, developed at Design Labor
in Bremerhaven, during the workshop led by
Gijs Bakker (1999), and designs from Hubert
Gasthaus (*Armed Candlestick*) and Lothar
Windels (the *Fritz* trolley), both created during
the workshop led by Ron Arad, Sebastian
Bergne and Konstantin Grcic at the Royal
College of Art in London (1999).

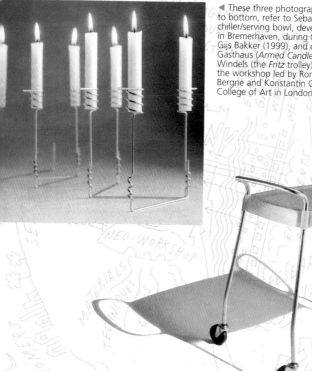

Memory Containers Creole Project

● The first metaproject coordinated by CSA, opening up Alessi to young designers; to be precise, young women designers, as during the introductory phase around 200 women designers under 30 were invited from all over the world. The questions we were asking: what is expected of the object? How are objects born, how do they change when moving from one culture to another? What changes in their shape, perception, use? How does an object become a cultural object? This was an exploration into the archetypes of presentation and "offering" of food and its rituals, with inspiration coming from the memory of a culture or a personal experience. The goal was to realize a "Creole" project, a test-tube cloning of that which, given its natural span, happens much more slowly when different cultures come together.

▲ *Treats* goodies box by Anna Gili (1998).

▼ The *Chimu* table centre-piece bowl by Joanna Lyle (1992).

▲ Pierced *Basket* by Susan Cohn (1992), also responsible for the *Cohndom Box* on the right (1999), the elegant and provocative holder for condoms.

◀ In the heat of the moment, *Inneres Feuer*, the chafing-dish with candle designed by Vera Purtscher (1997).

▼ *Tundra* is the poetic trivet with reindeer, designed by Kristiina Lassus (1995).

▲ Above, Clare Brass's three *Kalistò* kitchen boxes. Left, *Brasero*, a chafing-dish with candles, designed by Maria Sanchez (1992).

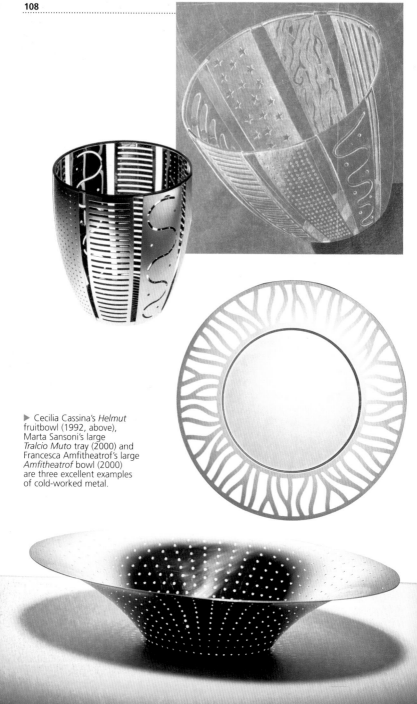

▶ Cecilia Cassina's *Helmut* fruitbowl (1992, above), Marta Sansoni's large *Tralcio Muto* tray (2000) and Francesca Amfitheatrof's large *Amfitheatrof* bowl (2000) are three excellent examples of cold-worked metal.

Memory Containers

cucchiaino per spezie in polvere

le foglie

◀ The relationship between steel and glass looms large in the Biological Project. Above, the *Oggetto dell'equilibrio* (1996) is the a set for perfuming and restoring balance to the home. Left, Pierangelo Caramia's *Bisquit box* and Theo Williams's *Honey pot* (1995). Below, Joanna Lyle's *Kitchen boxes,* and bottom, Alejandro Ruiz's *Parmenides* parmesan cheese grater (1994).

● This chapter examines a new vein of research: the discovery of Es, in a primary concept, of perception, more closely associated with intuition and receptive capabilities than the expression of different cultures through stylistic languages. The goal is to unearth new relationships linking the rule and the project: the living, vital object wins the man and nature conflict.

● The metaproject F.F.F., begun in 1991, grew out of a desire to explore the emotional structure of objects even more profoundly than we had done in the past. We were interested in the most delicate, intimate, sensory human needs. The objects became ludic tools, telling little tales, giving captivating twists to everyday uses, suggesting a mediation with playfulness… they become a bridge to the fantastical.

F.F.F. Family Follows Fiction

▲ The *Mix Italia* espresso coffee maker (1993) was one of the last joint projects by the King-Kong duo.

▶ Thanks to its allusive shape and the instinctive sense of empathy and familiarity it breeds, *Penguin Tea* with its special *Happy Egg* (1993), is one of F.F.F.'s symbol-objects. The objects by Venturini and Giovannoni in the picture above are also part of this research.

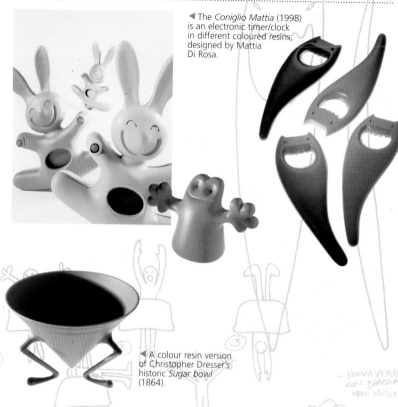

◀ The *Coniglio Mattia* (1998) is an electronic timer/clock in different coloured resins, designed by Mattia Di Rosa.

◀ A colour resin version of Christopher Dresser's historic *Sugar bowl* (1864).

— NUOVA VERSIONE CON BRACCIA E MANI MODIFICATE

For F.F.F. we drew upon Winnicott's words on "transitional objects", as well as Franco Fornari's "theory of emotional codes". At the outset the idea was to reproduce the process of creation and animation of the object common to the world of childhood, and to primitive cultures.

▶ The stars of this page are the amusing little devil *Bottle-openers* by Biagio Cisotti (1994), Mattia Di Rosa's laughing little creatures (*Timer/clock, Pressure caps, Kitchen boxes*).

ALESSI

▶ The *Bimboveloce* cakestand by Mattia di Rosa (1996), and *Miamor*, Enrica Zanzi's photo/message holder containing a secret compartment (1996).

▼ Another F.F.F. product/character, in production starting in 1998, is the *Folpo* (which in Veneto dialect means octopus, as can be seen from the tentacles of the little tame creatures) glass whisk cum measurer by Marta Sansoni.
Two fresh young designers: Gabriella Giandelli's *Ute* and *Loki* magnet/hooks, and Luca Bacelli's *Sister Clips* pegs (2000).

▼ Stefano Pirovano pursues his research into playful little sensorial design performances with his *Peppino* pepper grinder, *Salo* salt mill and *Te ò* (2000) tea strainer.

● As well as the kitchen, which in the last twenty years has provided food for thought for the vast majority of our designs, another part of the house, the bathroom, has gradually become one of the most intriguing growth areas for our domestic fantasy. It is interesting that this phenomenon has developed without manufacturers having too much to do with it: very few bathroom objects, large or small, are an expression of interesting, fun, poetic design. A few years ago we began to fill this gap. As well as the

Bagno

▼ With a burgeoning family of bright characters in thermoplastic rubber—*Rondo* cap for toothpaste tube, *Otto* interdental thread holder and *Sden* toothbrush cover—Stefano Pirovano (1998) has set his sights on bringing some fun to dental hygiene for children (and adults too).

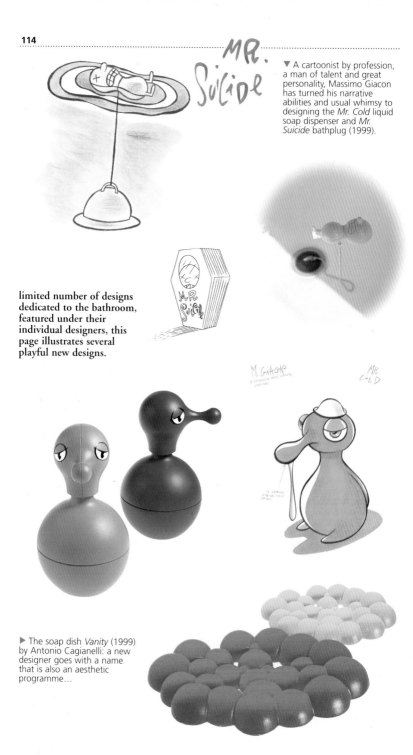

MR. Suicide

▼ A cartoonist by profession, a man of talent and great personality, Massimo Giacon has turned his narrative abilities and usual whimsy to designing the *Mr. Cold* liquid soap dispenser and *Mr. Suicide* bathplug (1999).

limited number of designs dedicated to the bathroom, featured under their individual designers, this page illustrates several playful new designs.

▶ The soap dish *Vanity* (1999) by Antonio Cagianelli: a new designer goes with a name that is also an aesthetic programme…

Stefano Giovannoni

" But who is this Michael Graves? He's certainly not a designer! "

● A "born again" designer par excellence, bearing a vague resemblance to a rumpled teddy bear, a man who looks like he might be anything except a much-acclaimed designer, Stefano conceals one of the most explosive talents I have ever had the good fortune to come across. He is not happy that we classify him as "one of the young", he feels he is destined for the designer hall of fame, and he wants to have his share of acclaim with my "masters". He'll no doubt get there, even if a little grizzly and impatient at times.

◀ The *Mary biscuit* boxes (1995) speak a soft, flowing language: with such sweet and soft dispositions, I am convinced that all Giovannoni's objects look at us affectionately with the mysterious yet warm smile of the *Mona Lisa*, "that smile associated with the sentiment of beauty which in adulthood moves the human heart, which for all of us, when falling in love or glimpsing a beautiful thing, is apparently associated with the intense visual relationship established with our mother's face, constituted as representative of the intra-uterine bliss" (Frontori, 1986).

◀ *Lilliput* (1993) is Giovannoni's highly original and inventive salt and pepper set. The two containers have magnetic feet which stick to the base.

ALESSI

▲ The *Nutty the Cracker* nutcracker (1993) is an example of how Giovannoni works, his finger on the pulse of our emotional codes, in particular that of the mother and child.

▲ *Gnam*: a cartoon-character name for the bread bin designed by Giovannoni in 2000. The cartoon inspiration is evident in the simple river pebble form, and in the extraordinary, brilliant transparency of the materials employed.

▼ *Fruit Mama*: a big, welcoming hand holding up the fruit, or is it a "new apple tree"? Definitely another non-anonymous presence in the house, which Giovannoni wishes to animate with a thousand characters of all hues (1993).

▲ *Happy Spices* is a family of little and dispensers for spices, salt and pepper (1997).

▲ The cartoon effect reaches its apogee with the infamous *Merdolino* (1993). Without pulling his punches, Giovannoni tackles an indispensable but "taboo" object, the toilet brush, turning it into a slender vase from which sprouts a long, allusive and inviting shrub.

▶ A few years on from the now-legendary *Merdolino*, which shocked the conventional stalwarts of design, Stefano has struck again at the same target—there's no more delicate way of putting it. His *Johnny the Diver* plunger (1999), soapdish and *Big Bubbles* toothbrush holder cup (1999) and the *Up-pill* make-up remover pad dispenser (2001) all confirm his vocation and interest in this area of the home that has all too often been ignored by design.

ALESSI

▶ The *Alibaba* (1998) jug with vacuum glass poses an intriguing question: why this particular name? Let's hazard a guess. In the cave of the forty thieves, the hero of this Oriental fairytale hides inside a rounded earthenware jar, from which the top of his turban pokes out: Stefano Giovannoni—a philologist of the fairy tale—is perhaps summoning up this image.

◀ Mnemonic references are far clearer for the *Rimini* cutlery drainer (1998). The visual pointer is explicit and heart-warming: that old bucket abandoned so many times on a beach with its spade and sand moulds.

▼ *Big Clip* (1998) and *Spank* (2000) pull a classic estrangement trick: changing the function of a common, everyday object by subverting its proportions. In this case, a humble paper clip and a children's game respectively become a photo holder and carpet beater.

◀ Ex-children may recall a small and well-loved cartoon character called Grisù, a little dragon always busy trying to remedy the damage caused by the fire he inadvertently breathes. We trust that those who get to grips with the long neck of this diminutive household dragon *Bruce*, will be more careful with this hot item, a table lighter (1998).

▲ *Cico* (2000) is another very recent example of Stefano's more figurative, anthropomorphic and zoomorphic narrative approach.

▲ Toothpicks may be indispensable, but they can be embarrassing to use: to put a light touch to what is not a particularly refined gesture, Giovannoni pulls out a rabbit from the unpredictable top hat of his creativity: the *Magic Bunny* toothpick holder (1998).

◀ "Macaroni, you've pushed me to the limit and now I'm going to eat you!" This is how Italian comic Alberto Sordi enjoined battle with a huge plate of steaming pasta. *Rigatone* is an invitation to eat Mediterranean-style, a kitchen box for spaghetti designed by Giovannoni (1998), whose shape and "topping" (a tomato lid) mimic what is probably Italy's best-known dish.

▶ *Ship Shape* (1998) is a creative container: it can be used for sauces, butter, jams… Sweet or savoury, it comes with a ready-to-use spatula for your imaginative delights.

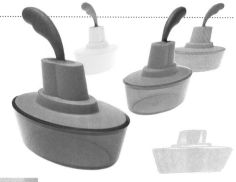

▼ An international character with a long-standing pedigree in texts on pedagogy and psychoanalysis, Pinocchio is now a long-nosed funnel, the smiling *Pino* (1998): truth or lie?

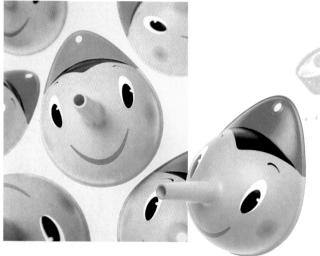

▶ Among so many festive eating rites, there is one lonely and melancholic pastime: breaking into a boiled egg, an act which is usually performed in reluctant intimacy, in a deep silence broken only by those tentative blows to the shell, making the humble boiled egg almost a metaphor for crepuscular solitude. Giovannoni has managed to brighten this moment up, make it a playful and gregarious thing with *Coccodandy* (1998), his basket for cooking eggs, which comes with four highly coloured recesses for cooking and serving eggs to friends.

Alessi. Extra ordinary.

◀ *Mami* (1999) is the third set of saucepans in the history of Alessi, after *La Cintura di Orione* by Sapper and *Falstaf* by Mendini. This time I entrusted to a young designer the difficult task of stimulating people's imagination by exploring the archaic world of "kitchenware". The spelt soup bubbles once again in the earthenware jar, and the capacious, rotund and sacred pots "with two ears" (as Catullus wrote) evoke the warmth of bygone eras. The truly complete set, in total harmony with Giovannoni's "poetics of the emotions", includes also the *Frying pans* and *Beafsteak pans* in non-stick cast aluminium.

Ethno

▼ *Ethno* (2000), conceived to be the new pop icon of the twenty-first century, has been made into objects from our most classic metal—stainless steel—with finely decorative results, and become a plastic range too (transmuted into neo-industrial North African items—right, the *Marrakesh* basket).

Guido Venturini

" Fields of expression such as art, music and cinema allow you to get out the nasty, ugly, violent things, because of their nature providing a release. Design does not usually offer such opportunities… "

● Guido is a committed explorer of the "Twilight Zone". His objects are highly expressive characters: wild, certainly out of the ordinary, vaguely monstrous but never threatening, indeed, to me they look like they're asking our assistance. Guido does a lot of thinking about the role of the designer in today's society, he is aware of the contradictions inherent in our work: I like seeing his work as that of a conscientious objector. Good old Guido, we'll travel far together, as long as you don't get lost along the way!

▼ This gas-lighter is called *Firebird* (1993), but the name is not a homage to Stravinsky. It is one of the most explicit and "courageous" of all the characters in the Alessi catalogue, an ironic reference to the "erotic code".

◄ The *Nonno di Antonio* garlic-squeezer.

▼ The china dishes, crystal glasses and steel and plastic cutlery of this complete *Dinner Service* make it the centrepiece of the Guido family. As is sometimes the case with our more complex projects, the gestation period for this one was long: six years of work. The results show the wait was worth it—once again, unmistakably, we are treated to the underlying theme of Venturini's poetics: the anthropomorphic and fetishistic iconography that hints at the "dark side", and the elegantly neo-primitive stylistic cues.

▶ *Pluto* china service and *Porthos* and *Acqua* glasses (2001).

▼ In stainless steel or in blue and yellow, the *Wardance* tray (1998) is decorated in a rather disconcerting manner: a perfect recipient for poisoned apples, it might help to bring back the historical position of taster.

◀ The *Fred Worm* jug with vacuum glass (1997). Guido's designs are so anthropomorphic that the other day we received an e-mail from Dallas, Texas, from a certain Fred Worm asking us to pay him a royalty for using his name…

▼ *Gino Zucchino* (1993) a sugar sifter, but at Alessi it has become so popular it has turned into a kind of garden gnome.

▲ *Inka* press filter coffee maker (2000). As with the cutlery, our designer and technicians have really applied themselves to using the latest plastics in an innovative way, drawing upon the extraordinary functional and sensorial qualities of this material—which remain evident as long as it not used in too "cheap" a way, so often the case with mass produced household goods.

ALESSI

▶ Faithful to his creative exploration of the shadowy corners of the unconscious, after a long gestation (due mainly to a lengthy sojourn in the Mexican desert), Spring 2000 sees the birth of one more character, the *Okkio!* table brush for removing crumbs and clothes brush for removing fluff.

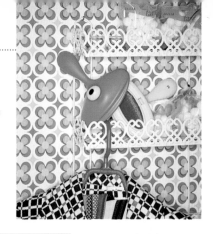

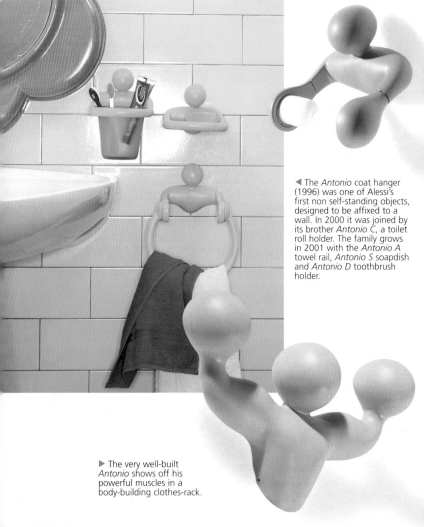

◀ The *Antonio* coat hanger (1996) was one of Alessi's first non self-standing objects, designed to be affixed to a wall. In 2000 it was joined by its brother *Antonio C*, a toilet roll holder. The family grows in 2001 with the *Antonio A* towel rail, *Antonio S* soapdish and *Antonio D* toothbrush holder.

▶ The very well-built *Antonio* shows off his powerful muscles in a body-building clothes-rack.

Historical Reproductions

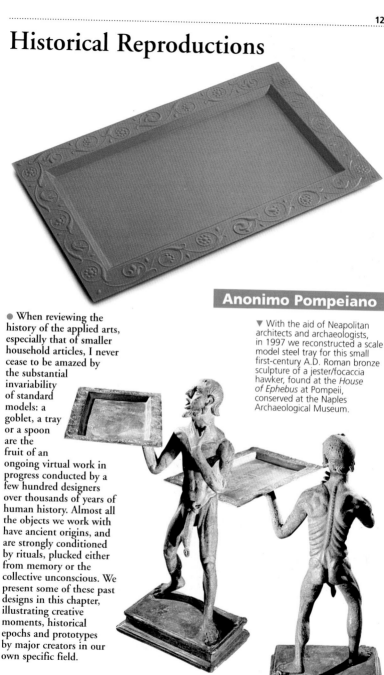

Anonimo Pompeiano

● When reviewing the history of the applied arts, especially that of smaller household articles, I never cease to be amazed by the substantial invariability of standard models: a goblet, a tray or a spoon are the fruit of an ongoing virtual work in progress conducted by a few hundred designers over thousands of years of human history. Almost all the objects we work with have ancient origins, and are strongly conditioned by rituals, plucked either from memory or the collective unconscious. We present some of these past designs in this chapter, illustrating creative moments, historical epochs and prototypes by major creators in our own specific field.

▼ With the aid of Neapolitan architects and archaeologists, in 1997 we reconstructed a scale model steel tray for this small first-century A.D. Roman bronze sculpture of a jester/focaccia hawker, found at the *House of Ephebus* at Pompeii, conserved at the Naples Archaeological Museum.

Christopher Dresser

▲ Dresser's many silver objects (the *Teapots*, the *Cruet sets*, the *Parmesan cheese-butter bowl with ice holder*) show he was always far ahead of his time.

● Dresser (1834–1904) was a well-regarded English botanist and scholar of the decorative arts who was probably the first industrial designer in the modern sense of the term. Unlike his Arts & Crafts Movement contemporaries, he wholeheartedly accepted all the implications of industrial mass-production, harnessing this to the design of bold, highly visionary crafted objects.

▶ This *Toast-rack* (1878), manufactured in stainless steel in 1991, has functional lines that are a foretaste of the Bauhaus spirit.

▲ Dresser was a prime example of the Moderate Transgression I seek in design. His projects show he knew the techniques of metal production better than any designer who has come to Alessi, and it is no coincidence that some of the objects we have chosen to "reproduce" are naturals for manufacture in modern day stainless steel.

This did not prevent him from never accepting the technical as a goal; he constantly probed boundaries as he sought higher expressive and constructive results. Some of these results, such as his *Triangular teapot* (designed in 1880 and produced in 1991) with legs, are even unsettling, while others show daring levels of intellectual and professional openness.

● Founded by Walter Gropius in Weimar in 1919 as a school of art and applied arts, subsequently directed by Hannes Meyer and Mies van der Rohe, Bauhaus is one of the historic workshops whose *mission* Alessi hopes to share. The reproductions on these pages are by Hans Przyrembel, Marianne Brandt, Otto Rittweger and Josef Knau. Because of the great talents of the people involved, because of its stated desire to develop a practice founded on the principle "Art and Engineering: a new unity" at the very moment the problem of reproducing works of art was a passionate topic of debate, because of the obstacles thrown up by conservative opponents and later by Nazism, Bauhaus was one of the legendary originators of the Modern Movement in architecture and design.

▶ The designs shown on these pages were created at the Bauhaus Metallwerkstatt between 1924 and 1930, prevalently under the tutelage of Lazló Moholy-Nagy (seen here with Marianne Brandt). They are manufactured under license from the Bauhaus Archiv in Berlin. On the facing page, the sleek *Tea doser* (Hans Przyrembel, 1926), *Sugar and creamer set* (Marianne Brandt and Helmut Schulze, 1926), and the *Set of two tea infusers* (Otto Rittweger and Josef Knau, 1924), all from 1995. In the middle, the *Tea and coffee service* (Marianne Brandt, 1924), manufactured in 1985.

▼ In a photo self-portrait which has become famous, Marianne Brandt, who made all the works on this page, "wears" metal items as if they were jewels.

ALESSI

▶ A leading figure in the shift to the modern in Finnish objects and architecture, Eliel Saarinen (1873–1950) had an organic and unitary vision of design: using simple geometric shapes (adapted, incidentally, from industrial processing) Saarinen broke a great deal of new ground with the concept of "domestic landscape". This silver *Tea set with urn*, we produced in 1987, is considered one of the archetypes of American design.

Eliel Saarinen

Piero Bottoni

◀ The *Modular element candies bowl* (1991), designed around 1928 is an exemplary Piero Bottoni piece: elegant rationalism, in no way self-satisfied, displaying clear classic lines yet totally practical. It is very moving to see an object made up of a cone and circle mutate into a living shape through the arrangement of its components.

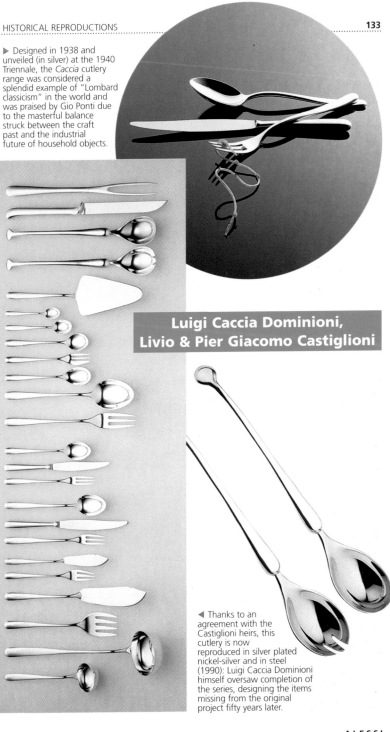

▶ Designed in 1938 and unveiled (in silver) at the 1940 Triennale, the *Caccia* cutlery range was considered a splendid example of "Lombard classicism" in the world and was praised by Gio Ponti due to the masterful balance struck between the craft past and the industrial future of household objects.

Luigi Caccia Dominioni, Livio & Pier Giacomo Castiglioni

◀ Thanks to an agreement with the Castiglioni heirs, this cutlery is now reproduced in silver plated nickel-silver and in steel (1990): Luigi Caccia Dominioni himself oversaw completion of the series, designing the items missing from the original project fifty years later.

ALESSI

Josef Hoffmann

● I think that if I had to pick just one designer out of the last century, it would have to be Josef Hoffmann. He founded the Wiener Werkstätte (1903) and left behind an immense body of work of extraordinary innovation, which has influenced generations of designers. That's not all: he was the first practitioner of a new way of working, in which the designer didn't work *for* but *with* an entrepreneur, influencing and inspiring his ventures, which has become the cornerstone of "Italy's design factories".

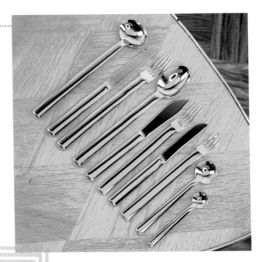

▲ At last, after all this time, Alessi finally has a "catering" design item! The *Rundes Modell* cutlery set, created in 1906 and manufactured by Alessi in 2000 under license from the Österreichisches Museum für Angewandte Kunst, was originally conceived for the legendary Cabaret Fledermaus in Vienna: a public place, a cabaret, a restaurant, really. Not just any old nightspot, though; it is not hard to imagine Schindler, Mahler, Schiele or even Sigmund Freud strolling in—a rather select clientele, a concentrate of creative minds the like of which rarely assembled in one place during the twentieth century. This is one of the cutlery designs that set the tone for the century.

◀ A brief comment on the unusual shape of the bowl of the tablespoon. In the original design, the bowl was set transversely to the handle, a very fetching solution ideal for sipping consommés, but not very practical for vegetable soups, or broths with pasta or rice. Together with Elisabeth Schmuttermeier, the curator at MAK, who helped us in our critical reconstruction, we made the decision to manufacture not just the original version but also a more contemporary—for want of a better word—version with a bowl coaxial to the handle.

The Alessi Museum

▲ Setting up an Alessi Museum is a physiological evolution in a two-decade-long process of theme and solution development. Many of the publications that have come out over this period presaged this outcome, if nothing else for the intrinsic, captivating poetic and artistic riches of this wealth of projects, for the density of intellectual debate from which they have emerged. Nevertheless, the Museum has opened its doors at a unique time, in a climate where the very function of museums is at a crossroads. The Museum is part of a phenomenon that is spontaneous and curious: Alessi is taking on the age/nature/identity of a museum, a novel kind of museum.

● Our role as a "Factory of Italian Design", somewhere between manufacturing and art, has gradually attracted the attention of museums of applied arts and industrial design from all over the world, and there have been many exhibitions of our work. Thanks to our constant experimentation over the years, we have produced a vast and fascinating body of prototypes which, together with our historical output and countless objects collected over the decades from all over the globe, form a valuable cross-section of the history of our field and our aims. The Alessi Museum, opened in spring 1998, has been built to house all the objects, designs, images and documents of all types regarding the history of Alessi and, more generally, the history of household articles. This new museum has come into being within our own structure; it is destined to reinforce our metaproject outlook and production policy (through the support of historical authorities), as well as provide a more direct and comprehensive channel for communicating with the museums we have been working with for some time. Designed by Mendini and curated by Francesca Appiani, the Alessi Museum is open to researchers, scholars, journalists and students.

ALESSI

MUSEO ALESSI

A.M 97

▼ Set up in a building inside the Crusinallo factory complex, the museum displays a huge number of prototypes, products no longer in production, graphics, blueprints and prints covering the history of Alessi. Also, machinery, engravings, designer installations, historic photos, books, magazines and catalogues. It is a veritable specialist museum of twentieth century applied art and design, with a number of very rare exhibits; what's more, it also serves as an ordered archive of Alessi's cultural identity.

◀ Year 2000: Mendini's *Merry-go-round of Wonders* at the Kunst- und Ausstellungshalle der Bundesrepublik Deutschland in Bonn was our way of taking up the invitation by Michael Erlhoof to feature in a major exhibition he was curating, comparing design in Germany and Italy during the second half of the twentieth century. The exhibition went under a soccer-inspired title "4-3", bringing up memories of a match Italians would prefer to forget.

▼ The Alessi Summer Festival was held in 1999 at the Forum in Omegna. The showcase event was the "Show of shows, twenty years of Alessi exhibitions", curated by the Atelier Mendini and Bruno Gregori. It comprised an anthology of the most significant moments from the many Alessi exhibitions over the years, providing an unusual glimpse of design utopias and trends, as well as indicating future directions of development.

SUMMER ALESSI FESTIVAL

◀ Alessandro Mendini has designed installations for various Alessi exhibitions: this page, left, the polymorphous organism for new products at the Milan showroom. Hans Hollein designed the display for the *Tea & Coffee Piazza* project (above) with the now famous split arch, as well as the major "Paesaggio casalingo" exhibition, presenting Alessi's output from 1921 to 1980, opening at the Milan Triennale in December 1979, travelling to Linz and Berlin in 1980.

ALESSI

▲ Pictures of Alessi exhibitions
in Caracas, Sydney, Paris, and
Tel Aviv recall the many shows
held in museums all over the
world: "Paesaggio casalingo"
(Milan, Linz, Berlin 1979–81);
"Tea & Coffee Piazza" (United
States, Milan, Krefeld, Zurich,
Aachen, Barcelona, Kyoto,
Ghent, Antwerp 1983–86);
"La Conica e altre caffettiere"
(Milan 1983); "Tafelarchitektur"
(Rotterdam, Düsseldorf 1985);
"Création" (Lyon 1986); "La
caffettiera e Pulcinella" (Milan
1987); "Not in production /
Next to production" (Milan,
Ghent 1988–90); "L'atelier
Alessi" (Paris, Brussels,
Scandinavia, Brazil, Zagreb

1989–95); "100% Make Up"
(Florence, Ghent, Groningen,
Roanne, Nice 1992–93); "Alessi
1921–1994" (France 1994);
Manger (Vevey 1994); "For the
sake of use" (Tel Aviv 1994);
"F.F.F." (Ljubljana 1995);
"Achille Castiglioni Designer"
(Barcelona-Milan-Bergamo-Weil
am Rhein-New York-Tokyo-
Niitsu-Breda 1995–98);
"Starckologie" (Frankfurt, Paris
1996); "Metallarbeiten" (Berlin
1996); "Omaggio ad Aldo
Rossi" (Milan-Hamburg 1998);
"Alessi" (New York 1998);
"Alessi, The Dream Factory"
(Caracas 1998); Alessi Summer
Festival, "Mostra delle Mostre"
(Omegna 1999).

The Wonder Shop

● As I have tried to convey in this book, our "dream factory" has, in the last eighty years, produced a catalogue of objects of a richness and complexity that is perhaps without equal in our industry: over 100 designers, 2,000 items, non-stop development of new projects, taking in a range of materials which, starting with our roots in metals, has gradually expanded to include plastics, wood, crystal, porcelain, appliances and consumer electronics. The large number of objects, not to mention the multitude of object types and different design approaches, means that extra special care is required in presenting them to the public. In the last few years it has become increasingly clear that as well as the many multi-brand stores around the world, it was a good idea to have exclusive Alessi stores, offering the best possible presentation and display of our wares. In 1997 I asked Atelier Mendini to develop a blueprint for "an ideal Alessi store". The fundamental concept was to handle Alessi objects as if they were fairy-tale characters, each with its own story and traits, and a desire to transmit joy and aesthetic energy. The interior design of these stores, which we are creating in a number of cities around the world, combines the excitement of fairy-tales with the effects of a *Wunderkammer*, the "Wonder Chamber" popular during the Renaissance and Baroque. These display locations have been devised to summarize the characters produced by the "dream

▲ The hallmark of the Mendini-designed Berlin *Flagship* (2000, Heike Both), located in the Stilwerk building in Kantstrasse 17—Mendini was also responsible for the Düsseldorf Flagship on the next page—is the important decorative motif in precious Bisazza mosaic tesserae, an Italian homage to the architectural renaissance of the German capital.

factory", and to convey a sense of adventure in design and the homescape. Spring 2001 sees Alessi *Flagships* in Milan (Enrico Corti, Corso Matteotti, 9), Hamburg, Berlin, Düsseldorf, Stockholm, Oslo, Helsinki, Strasbourg, Singapore (Lim Choon Hong, Penang 9), Tokyo, São Paolo (Noemia and Maurizio Roizen, Gabriel Monteiro da Silva 1903), Atlanta (Scott Reilly, 805 Peachtree Street), San Francisco (Cath Morrison

◀ The Düsseldorf *Flagship* (2000, Stefan Reichert), at 15 Grünstrasse.

▼ Following on from his Milan store, the Hamburg *Flagship* (1996, Marcus Rexter), located in the Stilwerk building, looking out onto the Baltic at 68 Grosse Elbstrasse, was our second store to be built along the lines of this new concept. The fact that Alessi has three *Flagships* in Germany is a sign of our attention towards this nation, which is the world's largest design market.

and Carol Bale Malcolm, 424 Sutter Street) and London (Jan Vingerhoets, 22 Brook Street). We have adhered to the same display concept for the shops-within-shops we are setting up in many of the world's finest multi-brand stores—the number is around 40 and growing.

▶ *Flagships* in Helsinki
at 39 Fredrikinkatu (1998,
Mikael and Anita Ruola), Oslo
at 6 Skovveien (1998, Tom
Howard), and Stockholm
at 20 Humlegardsgatan
(1995, John Baroi)—Alessi's
embassies to Scandinavia,
a region that is particularly
discerning when it comes
to good design.

▼ Strasbourg (1999, Jean-Pierre Ferry),
in Rue des Juifs no. 2, was the site our
first *Flagship* in France. This store was
entrusted with the demanding task
of promoting design in a country with
age-old and noble cultural traditions;
a country that is notoriously a little
hard to please when it comes to what
was once known as "style
contemporain"…

◀ For the Tokyo
Alessi Building (1999,
Shigeto Mutoh) in
Kita-Aoyama Minato-
ku, the first project
encompassing an
entire (diminutive as
it may be) urban
building, the Atelier
Mendini worked with
DNA similar to that
of the Crusinallo
factory, establishing
a kinship to span
the continents.
Our second Japanese
Flagship opened in
2000 at Tokyo Ikspiari
(2000, Shigeto
Mutoh).

ALESSI

Monographs

E. Sottsass, *Esercizio formale*, exhibition catalogue, Alessi, Crusinallo 1979.

A. Mendini, *Paesaggio casalingo. La produzione Alessi nell'industria dei casalinghi dal 1921 al 1980* (1st ed. Domus, Milan 1979), Internationales Design Zentrum, Berlin 1981.

F. Burkhardt, *Cibi e riti – Essen und Ritual*, proceedings of the design seminar held at the IDZ in Berlin in January 1981, Alessi, Crusinallo 1982 (1988[2]).

Var. Authors *Tea & Coffee Piazza*, with introduction by Alessandro Mendini, Shakespeare & Company, Milan 1983 (1986[5]).

A. Rossi, *"La conica", "La cupola" e altre caffettiere*, Alessi, Crusinallo 1984 (1988[3]).

Var. Authors, *Staedelschule*, Alessi, Crusinallo 1985.

E. Medagliani and F. Gosetti, *Pastario ovvero atlante delle paste alimentari italiane*, Alessi, Crusinallo 1985.

P. Scarzella, *Il bel metallo. Storia dei casalinghi nobili Alessi*, Arcadia, Milan 1985.

A. Alessi and A. Gozzi, *La cintura di Orione. Storia, tecnica e uso dei recipienti da cottura in metallo per la Grande Cucina*, Longanesi, Milan 1987.

R. Dalisi, *La caffettiera e Pulcinella. Ricerca sulla caffettiera napoletana 1979–1987*, Alessi, Crusinallo 1987 (1989[2]).

P. Scarzella, *Steel & Style. The Story of Alessi Houshold Ware*, Arcadia, Milan 1987.

A. Alessi, *Not in Production / Next to Production*, exhibition catalogue, Alessi, Crusinallo 1988.

A. Alessi and A. Gozzi, *La cucina Alessi*, Econ, Düsseldorf 1988.

L. Polinoro, *L'officina Alessi. Alberto Alessi e Alessandro Mendini: dieci anni di progetti, 1980–1990*, F.A.O./Alessi, Crusinallo 1989.

Var. Authors, *Philippe Starck*, F.A.O., Crusinallo 1990.

Var. Authors, *Christopher Dresser*, F.A.O., Crusinallo 1991.

Var. Authors, *Rebus sic…*, Centro Studi Alessi (ed.), with texts by A. Alessi, F. La Cecla, L. Leonini, M. Migliari, M. Pandolfi, L. Polinoro, L. Scaraffia, L. Vercelloni, F.A.O./Alessi, Crusinallo 1991.

A. Branzi, *Il dolce Stil Novo (della casa)*, F.A.O./Alessi, Crusinallo 1991.

R. Dalisi, *L'oggetto eroticomiko*, P. Scarzella (ed.), F.A.O./Alessi, Crusinallo 1991.

A. Mendini, *La fabbrica estetica*, F.A.O./Alessi, Crusinallo 1992.

Le fabbriche del design italiano. Alessi: une dynastie d'objets, exhibition catalogue, Istituto Italiano di Cultura di Parigi, Carte Segrete, Rome 1993.

L. Polinoro, *Family Follows Fiction*, F.A.O., Crusinallo 1993.

Var. Authors, *Alessi. The Design Factory, Academy Editions*, London 1994.

R. Poletti, *La cucina elettrica. I piccoli elettrodomestici da cucina dalle origini agli anni settanta*, Electa/Alessi, Milan 1994.

E. Mari, *Ecolo*, F.A.O., Crusinallo 1995.

B. Pedretti, *Opere postume progettate in vita. Metallwerkstatt Bauhaus anni '20 – anni '90*, Electa/Alessi, Milan 1995.

Var. Authors, *L'oggetto dell'equilibrio*, Electa/Alessi, Milan 1996.

M. Meneguzzo, *Philippe Starck distordre*, Electa/Alessi, Milan 1996.

G. Bertsch, *Der Wasserkessel von Michael Graves*, Verlag Form, Frankfurt 1997.

F. Burkhardt, J. Capella and F. Picchi, *Perché un libro su Enzo Mari*, Federico Motta Editore, Milan 1997.

S. Gronert, *Die Espressokanne von Richard Sapper*, Verlag Form, Frankfurt 1997.

Alessi. The Design Factory, Academy Editions, London 1998[2].

F. Sweet, *Alessi Art and Poetry*, Thames & Hudson, London 1998.

M. Collins, *Alessi*, Carlton Books Limited, London 1999.

M. Collins, *Alessi*, Bassermann, Niedernhausen 1999.

Selected Bibliography

XI Triennale, exhibition catalogue (Milan, Triennale), Milan 1957.

Carmelo Cappello, exhibition catalogue, Messina 1973.

XV Triennale, exhibition catalogue (Milan, Triennale), Milan 1973.

Dusan Dzamonja. Sculture, disegni e progetti dal 1963 al 1974, exhibition catalogue, Milan 1975.

A. Pansera, *Storia e cronaca della Triennale*, Longanesi, Milan 1978.

Design & Design, exhibition catalogue of the XI Compasso d'oro, ADI, Milan 1979.

XVI Triennale, exhibition catalogue (Milan, Triennale 1979–1982), Alinari, Florence.

Var. Authors, *Design ist unsichtbar*, exhibition catalogue, Löcker Verlag, Vienna 1980.

Centrokappa, Il design italiano negli anni '50, Domus, Milan 1980.

Diseñadores Industriales Italianos 1980, exhibition catalogue (Buenos Aires, Universidad de Buenos Aires, Faculdad de Arquitectura y urbanismo), Buenos Aires 1980.

A. Grassi and A. Pansera, *Atlante del design italiano 1940–1980*, Fabbri, Milan 1980.

B. Radice, *Elogio del banale*, Alchimia, Milan 1980.

Bio 9, Bienale Industrijskega Oblikovanja, exhibition catalogue, Bio, Ljubljana 1981.

XII Compasso d'oro, exhibition catalogue, Electa, Milan 1981.

A. Mendini, *Architettura addio*, Shakespeare & Company, Milan 1981.

Var. Authors, *Conseguenze impreviste – Arte, moda, design*, exhibition catalogue (Florence), Electa, Milan 1982, vol. III.

Var. Authors, *Gli anni trenta. Arte e cultura italiana*, exhibition catalogue, Mazzotta, Milan 1982.

Var. Authors, *Nuove intenzioni del design*, R.D.E., Milan 1982.

P. Arnell, T. Bickford and K. Vogel Wheeler, *Michael Graves. Buildings and Projects 1966–1981*, Rizzoli International, New York 1982.

V. Gregotti, *Il disegno nel prodotto industriale. Italia 1960–1980*, Electa, Milan 1982.

F. Irace, *Precursors of Post Modernism – Milano 1920–30's*, exhibition catalogue, The Architectural League, New York 1982.

Italian Re-Evolution, exhibition catalogue (La Jolla Museum of Contemporary Art), Milan 1982.

Provokationen – Design aus Italien. Ein Mythos geht neue Wege, exhibition catalogue (Hannover, Deutscher Werkbund), Hannover 1982.

Dal cucchiaio alla città nell'itinerario di 100 designer, exhibition catalogue, Electa, Milan 1983.

Design, exhibition catalogue (Zürich, Kunstgewerbe-Museum), Zürich 1983.

Design Experimenta Preview '83, exhibition catalogue, Todi 1983.

Design since 1945, exhibition catalogue (Philadelphia, Museum of Art), Rizzoli International, New York 1983.

Icsid design Milano, exhibition catalogue, R.D.E., Milan 1983, vol. IV.

C. Mann, *Clotet – Tusquets*, Gustavo Gili, Barcelona 1983.

A. Mendini, *Progetto infelice*, R.D.E., Milan 1983.

Var. Authors, *L'economia italiana tra le due guerre 1919–1939*, exhibition catalogue, Ipsoa, Rome 1984.

Bio 10, Bienale Industrijskega Oblikovanja, exhibition catalogue, Bio, Ljubljana 1984.

Castiglioni A. Meister des Design der Gegenwart, exhibition catalogue, Electa, Milan 1984.

Memphis Design, Kruithuis, s'Hertogebosch 1984.

Tre anni di design, XIII Compasso d'oro, exhibition catalogue, R.D.E., Milan 1984.

P. Arnell and T. Bickford, *Aldo Rossi. Buildings and Projects*, Rizzoli International, New York 1985.

A. Bangert, *Italienisches Möbeldesign. Klassiker von 1945 bis 1985*, Modernes Design, Munich 1985.

S. Bayley, *The Conran Dictionary of Design*, Conran Octopus, London 1985.

P.C. Bontempi and G. Gregori, *Alchimia*, Copi, The Hague 1985.

Dalla tartaruga all'arcobaleno, exhibition catalogue, (Milan, Triennale), Triennale-Electa, Milan 1985.

Ettore Sottsass, Mobili e qualche arredamento. Furniture and a few Interiors, exhibition catalogue, Mondadori-Daverio, Milan 1985.

H. Hollein, *Hans Hollein*, exhibition catalogue, A+U Publishing, Tokyo 1985.

R. Horn, *Memphis–Objects, Furniture and Patterns*, Running Press, Philadephia 1985.

S. Kohmoto, *Contemporary Landscape. From The Horizon of Post Modern Design*, exhibition catalogue (Kyoto, The National Museum of Modern Art), Kyoto 1985.

"Louisiana Revy", n. 3, 1985.

K. Sato, *Alchimia, Never Ending Italian Design*, Rikuyo-sha, Tokyo 1985.

R. Stern, *The International Design Yearbook 1985–1986*, Thames and Hudson, London 1985.

Strategie d'intesa, exhibition catalogue, Electa, Milan 1985.

H. Wichmann, *Die neue Sammlung. Ein neuer Museumstyp des 20. Jahrhunderts*, exhibition catalogue, Prestel, Munich 1985.

Var. Authors, *Les carnets du design. Les arts de la table*, Mad-Cap, Paris 1986.

E. Ambasz, *The International Design Yearbook 1986–1987*, Thames and Hudson, London 1986.

A table, exhibition catalogue (Paris, Centre Georges Pompidou), Paris 1986.

Bio 11, Bienale Industrijskega Oblikovanja, exhibition catalogue, Bio, Ljubljana 1986.

Caravelles. L'enjeu de l'objet, exhibition catalogue, Grenoble–Lyon–Saint-Etienne 1986.

A. Grassi and A. Pansera, *L'Italia del design. Trent'anni di dibattito*, Marietti, Casale Monferrato 1986.

Italia Diseño 1946–1986, exhibition catalogue (Museo Rufino Tamayo), Mexico 1986.

R. Krause, V. Pasca and I. Vercelloni, *La mossa del cavallo. Mobili e oggetti oltre il design*, Condé Nast, Milan 1986.

Semenzato Nuova Geri, asta di modernariato 1900–1986, Passigli, Milan 1986.

Teyssot, il progetto domestico. La casa dell'uomo: archetipi e prototipi, exhibition catalogue (Milan, XVII Triennale), Electa, Milan 1986.

Var. Authors, *The Post Modern Object*, exhibition catalogue, Ga Pindar, Londra 1987.

J. Capella and Q. Larrea, *Diseño de Arquitectos en los '80*, Gustavo Gili, Barcelona 1987.

M. Collins, *Towards Post-Modernism: Design since 1985*, British Museum Publications, London 1987.

Hans Hollein. Metaphores et metamorphes, exhibition catalogue (Paris, Centre Georges Pompidou), Paris 1987.

H. Klotz, *Jahrbuch für Architektur 1987–1988*, Deutches Architekturmuseum, Frankfurt 1987.

S. von Moos, *Venturi Rauch & Scott Brown*, Rizzoli International, New York 1987.

B. Munari, M. Bellin and A. Branzi, *Descendants of Leonardo da Vinci. The Italian Design*, Graphic-Sha, Tokyo 1987.

Nouvelles tendences. Les avant-gardes de la fin du XXe siècle, exhibition catalogue (Paris, Centre Georges Pompidou), Paris 1987.

XIV Premio Compasso d'oro, exhibition catalogue, Silvia, Milan 1987.

A. Rossi, *Aldo Rossi Architect*, Electa, Milan 1987.

D. Sudjic, *The International Design Yearbook 1987–1988*, Thames and Hudson, London 1987.

Var. Authors, *Alessandro Mendini*, exhibition catalogue (Groningen, Groninger Museum), Giancarlo Politi, Milan 1988.

Var. Authors, *Design und Wohnen*, exhibition catalogue, Helga Treft Verlag, Frankfurt 1988.

Var. Authors, *Sottsass Associates*, Rizzoli International, New York 1988.

Bio 12, Bienale Indusrijskega Oblikovanja, exhibition catalogue, Bio, Ljubljana 1988.

G. Bosoni and F.G. Confalonieri, *Paesaggio del design italiano 1972–1988*, Edizioni di Comunità, Milan 1988.

C. Colin, *Design d'aujourd'hui*, Flammarion, Paris 1988.

Id., *Starck*, Pierre Mardaga Editeur, Liège 1988.

Der Verzeichnete Prometheus, exhibition catalogue, Nishen Verlag, Berlin 1988.

Design in Catalogna, exhibition catalogue, BCD, Barcelona 1988.

I. Favata, *Joe Colombo, Designer 1930–1971*, exhibition catalogue, Idea Books, Milan 1988.

F. Fischer, *Design Heute*, exhibition catalogue (Frankfurt, Deutsches Architekturmuseum), Frankfurt 1988.

C. Gambardella, *Il progetto leggero. Riccardo Dalisi: vent'anni di design*, Clean, Napoli 1988.

F. Haks, *Alessandro Mendini Sketsboek – Sketches*, Froukje Hoekstra, Amsterdam 1988.

A. Isozaki, *The International Design Yearbook 1988–1989*, Thames and Hudson, London 1988.

B. Klesse, *Hundert Jahre Museum für Angewandte Kunst der Gegenwart. Mäzenatentum*, exhibition catalogue (Cologne, Museum für Angewandte Kunst), Cologne 1988.

La caffettiera napoletana e Pulcinella, exhibition catalogue (Taranto, Circolo Italsider), Editrice Scorpione, Taranto 1988.

R. Sambonet, *L'arte in tavola*, Industria Grafica Ronda, Milan 1988.

S. San Pietro and M. Vercelloni, *Nuovi negozi a Milan*, L'Archivolto, Milan 1988.

P. Sparke, *Italienisches Design*, Thames and Hudson, London 1988.

Richard Sapper. 40 Progetti di Design 1958–1988, exhibition catalogue, Arti Grafiche Mazzucchelli, Milan 1988.

H. Wichmann, *Italian Design 1945 bis heute*, Die Neue Sammlung, Munich 1988.

Var. Authors, *Alessandro Mendini*, exhibition catalogue, Giancarlo Politi, Milan 1989.

Var. Authors, *From Matt Black to Memphis and back again*, Blueprint/Wordsearch, London 1989.

Var. Authors, *Role of Design, V. Design for a Coming Age*, JIDPO, Tokyo 1989.

Var. Authors, *Von Außen von Innen. 25 Modus Jahre*, Modus Möbel, Berlin 1989.

M. Collins and A. Papadakis, *Post-Modern Design*, Rizzoli International, New York 1989.

P. and R. Colombari, *Effetto acciaio*, exhibition catalogue, Arti Grafiche Giacone, Turin 1989.

Compasso d'oro. Italian Design, exhibition catalogue, Silvia Editore, Milan 1989.

G. Lueg, *Design*, exhibition catalogue (Cologne,

Museum für Angewandte Kunst), Cologne 1989.

L. Peel, P. Powell and A. Garrett, *An Introduction to 20th Century Architecture*, Quinted Publishing, London 1989.

XV Premio Compasso d'oro, exhibition catalogue, Silvia Editrice, Milan 1989.

Var. Authors, *Michael Graves. Buildings and Projects, 1982–1989*, Princeton Architectural Press, Princeton 1990.

A. Bangert and K.M. Armer, *Design der 80er Jahre*, Bangert Verlag, Munich 1990.

N. Bellati, *New Italian Design*, Rizzoli International, New York 1990.

M. Bellini, *The International Design Yearbook 1990–1991*, Thames and Hudson, London 1990.

Collezione per un modello di museo del disegno industriale italiano, exhibition catalogue, Fabbri, Milan 1990.

European Community Design Prize 1990, exhibition catalogue, BCD, Barcelona 1990.

L. Gobbi, F. Morace, R. Brognara and F. Valente, *I Boom*, Lupetti & Co., Milan 1990.

W. Halen, *Christopher Dresser*, Christies, Oxford 1990.

J. Capella and Q. Larrea, *Oscar Tusquets objets dans le parc*, exhibition catalogue, Gustavo Gili, Barcelona 1990.

Metall für den Gaumen, exhibition catalogue, beim Herausgeber, Vienna 1990.

J. Myerson and S. Katz, *Kitchenware*, Conran Octopus, London 1990.

A. Rowland, *Bauhaus Source Book*, Quarto, London 1990.

Var. Authors, *Aldo Rossi Architecture 1981–1991*, Princeton Architectural Press, Princeton 1991.

Var. Authors, *Architetture elettriche*, Biticino, Milan 1991.

Var. Authors, *New and Notable Product Design*, Rockport Publishers, Rockport 1991.

A. Branzi, *Il dolce Stil Novo (della casa)*, F.A.O., Crusinallo 1991.

J. Capella and Q. Larrea, *Nuevo diseño español*, Gustavo Gili, Barcelona 1991.

O. Boissiere, *Starck*, Taschen Verlag, Cologne 1991.

S. Casciani and G. Di Pietrantonio, *Design in Italia 1950–1990*, Giancarlo Politi, Milan 1991.

2e Quadriennale Internationale de Design, exhibition catalogue, Caravelles 2, Lyon 1991.

P. Dormer, *The Illustrated Dictionary of Twentieth Century Designers*, Quarto Publishing, London 1991.

Formes des metropoles – Nouveaux designs en Europe, exhibition catalogue (Paris, Centre Georges Pompidou), Paris 1991.

P. Polato, *Il modello nel design*, Hoepli, Milan 1991.

Primavera del disseny. Barcelona 1991 Spring Design, exhibition catalogue (Barcelona, Ajuntament de Barcelona), Barcelona 1991.

Var. Authors, *Carl Larsson*, Bokforlaget Bra Bocker, Göteborg 1992.

Var. Authors, *Objects and Images*, U.I.A.H., Helsinki 1992.

Casa Barcelona, exhibition catalogue, IMPI, Barcelona 1992.

A. Ferlenga, *Aldo Rossi Architetture 1988–1992*, Electa, Milan 1992.

Nuovo bel design, exhibition catalogue, Electa, Milan 1992.

Starck in Wien, exhibition catalogue, Die Kommode, Vienna 1992.

M.C. Tommasini and M. Pancera, *Il design italiano*, Mondadori, Milan 1992.

Var. Authors, *Modern Ad Art Museum*, Stern, Hamburg 1993.

U.·Brandes, *Richard Sapper*, Steidi, Göttingen 1993.

B. Fitoussi, *Objects Affectifs*, Hazan, Paris 1993.

Cristina Morozzi, Massimo Morozzi, L'Archivolto, Milan 1993.

Design und Wohnen 2, exhibition catalogue, Helga Treft Verlag, Frankfurt 1993.

P. Dormer, *Design since 1945*, Thames and Hudson, London 1993.

H. Höger, *Ettore Sottsass Jun.*, Ernst Wasmuth, Berlin 1993.

Il design degli oggetti, exhibition catalogue (Gallarate, Civica Galleria d'Arte Moderna), Gallarate 1993.

La fabbrica estetica, exhibition catalogue, ICE, Milan 1993.

Museum für Angewandte Kunst. Ein Wegweiser von A bis Z, Cologne 1993.

S. Prinz, *Besteck des 20. Jahrhunderts*, Klinkhardt & Biermann, Munich 1993.

S. Borek, *The International Design Yearbook*, Rick Poynor, London 1993.

Richard Sapper Design, exhibition catalogue (Cologne, Museum für Angewandte Kunst), Cologne 1993.

M. Turinetto, *Dizionario del design*, Lupetti & C., Milan 1993.

Var. Authors, *Atelier Mendini. Una utopia visiva*, Fabbri, Milan 1994.

Arts et formes ou 40 variations pour une histoire d'eau, exhibition catalogue (Paris, Musée du Louvre), Paris 1994.

A. Buch and M. Vogt (ed.), *Janet Abrams, Laura Cerwinske, Michael Collins, Rainer Krause, Aldo Rossi, Michael Graves. Designer Monographs 3*, Vogt, Ernst & Son, Berlin 1994.

M. Byars, *The Design Encyclopedia*, Laurence King,

London 1994.

F. Burkhardt, *Marco Zanuso*, Federico Motta, Milan 1994.

T. Heidert, M. Stegmann, and R. Zey, *Lexikon Internationales Design*, Rowohlt, Hamburg 1994.

Raymond Guidot, histoire du design 1940, Hazan, Paris 1994.

The International Design Yearbook 1994, Laurence King, London 1994.

Totocchio, exhibition catalogue, F&T Boo, Vicenza 1994.

O. Tusquets Blanca, *Mas que discutible*, Tusquets Editores, Barcelona 1994.

A La Castiglione, exhibition catalogue, Istituto Italiano di Cultura, Barcelona 1995.

Das International Design Jahrbuch 1994–1995, Bangert Verlag, Munich 1995.

XVII Premio Compasso d'oro, exhibition catalogue, Silvia Editrice, Milan 1995.

Oscar Tusquets Enric Miralles, exhibition catalogue, Tusquets Editores, Barcelona 1995.

A. Pansera, *Dizionario del design italiano*, Cantini, Milan 1995.

Pour un couteau. design et couverts 1970–1990, exhibition catalogue, Thiers 1995.

The Hannover Yearbook of Industrial Design, exhibition catalogue (Hannover, Industrial Forum Design), Hannover 1995.

The Internationel Design Yearbook 1995, Laurence King Publishing, London 1995.

Thomas Haufe. Design, Dumont, Cologne 1995.

Torino design. Dall'automobile al cucchiaino, exhibition catalogue, Umberto Allemandi, Turin 1995.

Var. Authors, *Design im Wandel*, Bangert Verlag, Bremen 1996.

Var. Authors, *Dictionnaire International des Arts Appliques et du Design*, Editions du Regard, Paris 1996.

Alessandro Mendini 30 colours, V+K Publishing, Bussum 1996.

A. Branzi, *Il design italiano 1964–1990*, exhibition catalogue, Electa, Milan 1996, pp. 24, 243–45, 294, 309, 358, 360, 378, 383, 385.

S. Casciani, *The Art Factory*, exhibition catalogue, Editrice Abitare Segesta, Milan 1996.

F. Ferrari, *Ettore Sottsass, tutta la ceramica*, Umberto Allemandi, Turin 1996.

F. Haks, *Mendini*, L'Archivolto, Milan 1996.

M. Meuth and B. Neuner-Duttenhofer, *Piemont und Aostatal*, Droemer Knaur, Munich 1996.

A. Rossi, *Villa sul Lago Maggiore*, Il Cardo, Venezia 1996.

P. Starck, *Vanity Case*, Taschen, Cologne 1996.

The International Design Yearbook 1996, Laurence King, London 1996.

Werkzeuge. Design des Elementaren, Landesgalerie, Austria 1996.

Bella forma, Landschaftsverband Westfalen-Lippe, Hagen 1997.

F. Burkhardt and C. Morozzi, *Andrea Branzi*, Dis Voir, Paris 1997.

Gout Design, Musée de Louviers, Paris 1997.

S. Gronert, *The 9090 Cafetiere by Richard Sapper*, Verlag Form, Frankfurt 1997.

Var. Authors, *The International Design ·Yearbook 1998*, Laurence King Publishing, London 1998.

T. Hauffe, *Design. A coincise history*, Laurence King, London 1998.

Industridesign Igår og Idag, Henie Onstad Kunstsenter, 1998.

C. Morozzi, *Oggetti Risorti*, Costa & Nolan, Milan 1998.

M. Fortis, *Il made in Italy*, Il Mulino, Bologna 1998, pp. 110, 111, 112, 113.

A. Alessi, *La fabbrica dei sogni*, Electa, Milan 1999.

S. Annicchiarico (ed.), *I luoghi del caffè*, Editoriale Modo and Lavazza, Milan-Turin 1999.

J. Carmel-Arthur, *Philippe Starck*, Carlton, London 1999.

E. Gesine Baur, *Was Kommt, was bleibt. Die prognosen für das nächste Jahrtausend von…*, Deutscher Taschenbuch Verlag, Munich 1999.

Kunsthistorisches Institut der Universität Zürich und Autoren, *Georges-Bloch-Jahrbuch 1999*, Zürich 1999.

Industry Forum Design Award 1999, Hannover 1999, p. 93.

C. Neumann, *Design in Italia*, Rizzoli, Milan 1999.

A. Scevola, S. San Pietro, *Prodotto industriale italiano contemporaneo*, L'Archivolto, Milan 1999.

The International Design Yearbook, Laurence King Publishing, London 1999, pp. 8, 126, 131, 132, 212, 214.

S. Bayley, *Smag Taste*, Danish Design Centre, Copenhagen 2000.

V. Briatore with Map and Random, *Restyling. Meraviglie e miserie del progetto contemporaneo*, Castelvecchi 2000.

C. and P. Fiell, *Design del XX secolo*, Taschen, Cologne 2000.

C. Lloyd Morgan, *Starck*, Rizzoli, Milan 2000.

C. Lloyd Morgan, *20th century design: a reader's guide*, Architectural Press, Oxford 2000.

C. Piras, E. Medagliani, *Culinaria Italia. Italianische spezialitäten*, Könemann, Cologne 2000.

Alessi Objects in Museum Collections
and Public Institutions

Stedelijk Museum, Amsterdam; Museo de Artes Decorativas, Barcelona; Bauhaus-Archiv, Museum für Gestaltung, Berlin; Kunstgewerbemuseum SMPK, Berlin; National Gallery of Australia, Canberra; The Denver Art Museum, Denver; Kunstmuseum Düsseldorf, Düsseldorf; Museum Folkwang, Essen; Museum für Kunsthandwerk, Frankfurt; Museum voor Sierkunst, Gand; Design and Applied Art (Mudesa), Garabaer (Islanda); Israel Museum, Jerusalem; Groninger Museum, Groningen; Museum of Applied Arts, Helsinki; Louisiana Museum of Modern Art, Humlebaek; Kunstgewerbemuseum, Cologne; Museum für Angewandte Kunst, Cologne; The National Museum of Modern Art, Kyoto; Bio Design Collection, Ljubljana; Victoria and Albert Museum, London; National Gallery of Victoria, Melbourne; The Minneapolis Institute of Arts, Minneapolis; Die Neue Sammlung, Staatliches Museum für Angewandte Kunst, Munich; Yale University Art Gallery, New Haven; The Brooklyn Museum, New York; The Metropolitan Museum of Art, New York; The Museum of Modern Art, New York; Ostfriesisches Tee-Museum, Norden; Henie Instad Art Center Kunstsenterhovikodden, Norway; Museum of Applied Art, Oslo; Musées des Arts Décoratifs, Paris; Philadelphia Museum of Art, Philadelphia; Museum Boymans-van-Beuningen, Rotterdam; Museu de Arte, São Paolo; Deutsches Klingenmuseum, Solingen; Powerhouse Museum, Sydney; MAK Österreichisches Museum für Angewandte Kunst, Vienna; Kunstgewerbemuseum der Stadt Zürich, Zürich; Museum für Gestaltung, Zürich.

Photograph Credits

Holders of rights to any unidentified photographic material are invited to bring the matter to the attention of the originating publishers.

This book was printed by Elemond S.p.a.
at Mondadori Printing S.p.a., Verona, in the year 2001